Soul Medicine for a Fractured World

Healing, Justice, and the Path of Wholeness

LIZA J. RANKOW

ORBIS BOOKS
Maryknoll, New York 10545

Founded in 1970, Orbis Books endeavors to publish works that enlighten the mind, nourish the spirit, and challenge the conscience. The publishing arm of the Maryknoll Fathers and Brothers, Orbis seeks to explore the global dimensions of the Christian faith and mission, to invite dialogue with diverse cultures and religious traditions, and to serve the cause of reconciliation and peace. The books published reflect the views of their authors and do not represent the official position of the Maryknoll Society. To learn more about Maryknoll and Orbis Books, please visit our website at www.orbisbooks.com.

Manufactured in the United States of America

Library of Congress Cataloging-in-Publication Data

Names: Rankow, Liza J. author
Title: Soul medicine for a fractured world : healing, justice, and the path of wholeness / Liza J. Rankow.
Description: Maryknoll, NY : Orbis Books, [2025] | Includes bibliographical references and index. | Summary: "An integrative path toward healing and social transformation helping readers become agents of change"—Provided by publisher.
Identifiers: LCCN 2025027010 (print) | LCCN 2025027011 (ebook) | ISBN 9781626986374 trade paperback | ISBN 9798888660928 epub
Subjects: LCSH: Spirituality | Healing—Religious aspects | Social justice—Religious aspects
Classification: LCC BL624 .R373 2025 (print) | LCC BL624 (ebook)
LC record available at https://lccn.loc.gov/2025027010
LC ebook record available at https://lccn.loc.gov/2025027011

ADVANCE PRAISE FOR
Soul Medicine for a Fractured World

"This is a book of wisdom gleaned from a life lived from the core of the heart."

—**Alice Walker**, author, *The Color Purple*
and *In Search of Our Mothers' Gardens*

"The work is breathtaking, informative, and deeply reflective of the expansiveness of Rankow's spirituality. An amazing contribution to the field."

—**Barbara A. Holmes**, author, *Joy Unspeakable*
and *Crisis Contemplation*

"Within the great chasm of upheaval and uncertainty, we can forge the necessary skills to build toward a world more whole for us all. True to the wisdom of mystics throughout the ages, Liza Rankow offers an array of paths for us to walk in our unique way, together. For who amongst us does not need such life-nourishing medicine?"

—**Rev. angel Kyodo williams, Rōshi**, co-author
Radical Dharma: Talking Race, Love and Liberation

"*Soul Medicine* is a balm for the weary, a guide for the searching, and a radiant vision of hope for our shared future. With the wisdom and tenderness of a spiritual elder, Liza Rankow accompanies us on a journey of personal transformation and collective healing, reminding us of what becomes possible when spirit and justice meet. What a profound gift she has given the world."

—**Jen Bailey**, author, *To My Beloveds*
founder, Faith Matters Network

"*Soul Medicine* is a treasure—a profound solace and guide to navigate these difficult and tumultuous times. The author's lived experience shines through to offer grounding, humility, and grace."

—**Nina Simons**, author, *Nature, Culture, and the Sacred*
co-founder, Bioneers

"Deep in our soul, we know that healing the brokenness of the world is tied to our own spiritual growth. Liza Rankow's *Soul Medicine for a Fractured World* is a profound meditation on how to have love and healing spill out, over and over again, washing the whole world over. It is a book not only to be read, but taken to heart."

—**Omid Safi**, author, *Radical Love:
Teachings from the Islamic Mystical Tradition*

"In *Soul Medicine for a Fractured World*, Liza Rankow offers us a blessed opportunity to seize this apocalyptic moment of death and rebirth, to reimagine the in-between spaces of our personal dreams and worldly hopes, for an expansive healing and restoration of this terrestrial space that we call home."

—**Walter E. Fluker**, author, *Ethical Leadership*
director, The Howard Thurman Papers Project

"In the midst of chaos and collapse, Rankow invites us to restore a kind of wholeness that comes from an ancestral and insightful awareness of our soul's wisdom. We have the medicine within us for the wounds systemically inflicted upon us."

—**Zenju Earthlyn Manuel, Oshō**, author
Opening to Darkness and *The Way of Tenderness*

CONTENTS

Introduction vii

Part One: The Portal

   1. Crucible of the In-Between 3

   2. The Purpose of Our Living 15

   3. Thresholds of Initiation 27

Part Two: Restoring Wholeness

   4. The Medicine in Our Wounds 45

   5. Soul Care 60

   6. Healing Across Time 78

Part Three: Healing Separation

   7. Mystic Oneness & the World of Dualism 93

   8. Mystic Activism 108

   9. Healing Whiteness. 122

Part Four: A Wider Belonging

   10. Life, Death, Ancestors & Coming Generations 139

   11. Deep Listening .152

   12. Dream & Imagine. 167

   13. Healing the Soul of the World. 183

Additional Spiritual & Healing Practices. 195

Notes. 207

Acknowledgments. 223

Index of Spiritual & Healing Practices 225

All around us worlds are dying and new worlds are being born; all around us life is dying and life is being born. The fruit ripens on the tree, the roots are silently at work in the darkness of the earth against a time when there shall be new leaves, fresh blossoms, green fruit. Such is the growing edge! It is the extra breath from the exhausted lung, the one more thing to try when all else has failed, the upward reach of life when weariness closes in upon all endeavor. This is the basis of hope in moments of despair, the incentive to carry on when times are out of joint and men have lost their reason, the source of confidence when worlds crash and dreams whiten into ash. Look well to the growing edge!

Howard Thurman, *Meditations of the Heart*

INTRODUCTION

THIS BOOK IS ABOUT POSSIBILITY in the midst of crisis and upheaval.

We stand at a threshold. The structures of a world built on domination and division are crumbling, but still fighting to hold on. Each day brings news of worsening ecological, political, and social collapse. It can be tempting to disconnect in order to ease the intensity of the pain, to distract or numb ourselves in all the ways we do. The answer, however, is not to disconnect, but to connect more deeply. To find strength in something more powerful than the chaos: our belonging to a wholeness that is ancient, infinite, and eternal. We can engage the transformative potentials within the upheaval as a portal into another way of being. We can live with purpose and meaning, not just in spite of the rising tide of calamities around us, but as our *response* to them. When old worlds are dying, new ones can be born. That is the real opportunity available to us in these times.

What are the spiritual insights, the practices and capabilities we need to support us through this process? Who are the companions and teachers to guide us? How do we give ourselves as agents of collective liberation? And who are we called to become along the way?

At the heart of this book is healing. It explores both our personal wounds and places of growth, and our ancestral, societal, and global ones arising from centuries of injustice. They are intimately joined, and we must attend to both. Healing—

whether physical, emotional, or relational—is fundamentally about restoring wholeness. And social justice is a matter of restoring wholeness to individuals and communities where systematic and state-sanctioned harm has been done. Healing is an ongoing embodied practice, a process not a destination. There are many ways to approach this, of course, but I see it as profoundly spiritual work, animated by a wisdom and a power greater than our finite human selves.

Too often healing and spiritual growth are seen as separate from issues of justice. That fracture is part of the underlying cause of the challenges we face. Our wholeness is found in the integration of inner and outer, personal and collective, self and planet. Without this, any progress we make toward a just and harmonious world cannot endure. Unless our consciousness is changed, we will revert back to the patterns of domination and extraction that are rapidly leading to our demise. A social revolution alone is not enough; a spiritual revolution is also necessary. We must *become* the people who can sustain a reimagined society.

Foundations, Teachers & Roots

Soul Medicine for a Fractured World grows out of many decades of study, struggle, and practice. My lifework—and this book—stands on the shoulders of those through the generations who have served justice movements as healers, spiritual guides, and counselors. In these pages you will meet some of the teachers and comrades whose wisdom has shaped me. Two that have had a particularly profound impact on my formation are Dr. Howard Thurman and Brother Ishmael Tetteh. Both are socially engaged mystics, deeply rooted in the spirituality of Nature.

You'll meet others here as well: poets, visionaries, and those I call "mystic-activists"—people like Thich Nhat Hanh, Vimala

Thakar, Gloria Anzaldúa, and Malidoma Somé. Beneath the particulars of their faith, culture, or areas of social engagement lies a common pulse. Each has felt the essential oneness within all existence, and been moved by that intuition to work for justice, peace, and the well-being of all. These teachers invite us into an expansive communion with the sacredness found in all of Life. This worldview of oneness, held by mystics and Indigenous peoples throughout the ages, has profound applications for how we relate with one another and the Earth. We'll turn to these mentors from a variety of traditions to reveal an inspiring direction for social transformation, and consider what mystic activism might look like in our own lives.

The intersection of mystic spirituality and social action was the focus of my doctoral studies, but really, it has been the foundation of my life. As a child during the US war on Vietnam I was a precocious activist, "publishing" what I thought of as an underground pacifist newspaper, *The Dove*, and distributing it covertly to my third-grade class and the bus driver who carried us to school each day.

My parents, although vaguely liberal, were not involved in activist issues. Nor were they particularly religious. My father was raised as a mostly nonobservant Jew in the Bronx, his parents Ashkenazi immigrants from Ukraine (then part of the Russian Empire) and England. My mother, raised Lutheran in a largely Swedish immigrant community in Massachusetts, was no longer practicing much of anything.

What I remember most growing up were the books. I was nurtured in a climate of intellectual and spiritual seeking. No religious teachings. No institutional or doctrinal framing. Just shelves and shelves of books. I was nine the summer I read Paramahansa Yogananda's *Autobiography of a Yogi*. At ten or eleven, I went through a period of rising at 5 a.m. before school and reading the Gospels in my mother's weathered leather-bound confirmation Bible, as captivated by Jesus as I had been by Yogananda.

For many years I lost sight of that integration of spirit and justice my child-self so naturally understood. My life became a roller coaster—alternating cycles of intense activism, crash-and-burn health crises, and long periods of spirit-centered recovery. But each of these conditions also became my teachers. Over the decades, I found my way back (or perhaps forward) toward a life of balance. I began to live into the synthesis of activism, spirituality, and healing that we will explore together here.

Today, in my 60s, there's a way that I feel closer to that little girl than I do to all the years between then and now. As a child I heard the voice of Spirit, loved Nature and creativity, had a heart for justice. Now, as I come into elderhood, I hope to be more and more like that precious little one, but seasoned by the insight of my days. I pray to be faithful to the purpose and calling for my life. To make a meaningful difference in the lives of others. To pour myself out so fully that when I leave this Earth I have no regrets of things left undone. This is what I want for all of us, and it is one of the motivations for my writing this book.

Our Journey Together

Perhaps there is a wise-child within you, as well, calling you to a truth that has been forgotten. Or maybe there are other clues to your gifts and purpose scattered throughout your life. It's never too late (or too early!) to find them and seek out their message.

In these pages we will talk about purpose, and its importance as a compass through times of upheaval. We'll also look at healing in relationships, working with trauma, and finding the medicine in our wounds. We'll examine the ideological construction of oppression, and consider models of transformative social change that imagine a future of collaborative flourishing.

The times we inhabit have ushered us into a portal of individual and collective initiation. Part One of this book helps locate us as we navigate the tumult, and looks at how the archetype of initiation offers a framework that can lead us to our soul's wisdom. Parts Two and Three are about healing our personal, planetary, and ancestral wounds, and the conditions of social division that arise from them. In Part Four we (re)discover our inherent belonging to all of Life in a community that extends across generations and galaxies, and consider how we can move toward a world that honors that belonging.

Throughout this book are a number of spiritual and healing practices to help you put the ideas shared here into embodied action in your own life. Together we will engage deep listening—tuning into inner guidance, the wisdom of Nature and ancestors, and the vision of coming generations. We'll explore how to expand self-care into soul care, and how to work with emotions as allies in our healing. We'll weave back and forth from microcosmic to macrocosmic, personal to collective. Reflection questions will encourage you to surface further insights on the subjects we discuss.

At times it may seem like I am circling back to a topic, but that is the nature of life and growth. It isn't linear. We layer our learnings and link them to past experience, making bridges that enrich our understanding. Truly, it is *all* connected, because everything in Life is connected. Everything is part of the sacred wholeness. Everything is our teacher—or can be.

Thank you for joining me on this journey. May you find something here to nourish your spirit through the crucible of these times, and support you in bringing your own unique medicine to the world.

PART ONE

The Portal

A liminal space of formation and transformation …
A passage from one world to the next.

Transitions can only take place if we are willing to let go of what we have known, the worlds we have created, and our assumptions about 'how things are.' To let go is the precursor to being reborn.

—Barbara A. Holmes

In these prophetic times where human beings are pushing the Earth Mother's life support systems to the brink, it is imperative to do whatever is possible to elevate human consciousness. We must heal the separation from self, others and Mother Earth. This separation is the root cause for all the human dysfunctions that are destroying Mother Earth and ourselves.

—Kuuyux Ilarion Merculieff

People want creation without destruction. People want rebirth, but they don't want death.

—Sonya Renee Taylor

———————— ◎ ————————

1

Crucible of the In-Between

I SIT IN THE GATHERING DARKNESS, candle lit, offering prayers that I hope will somehow make a difference. I imagine them flying out my window like numinous birds, traveling through the streets of Oakland and out into the ethers where they join other prayers, join chants and spells and longings and wishes from every corner and continent, forming a murmuration of loving magic to enfold the planet. Prayers streaming ribbons of color, like the sunset now painted across the sky, or falling like tender rain to nourish parched ground. I send prayers on the wind to enter the nostrils

3

of every breathing soul upon this Earth, to root themselves like stubborn seeds in every heart and mind. May they grow, these prayer-seeds, may they flourish and flower and bear healing fruit.

These are desperate times. Times of dying worlds and decaying empires. The fires of division fuel increasingly frequent acts of racist terrorism and state violence. Massive wealth is concentrated among a small group of elites, while poverty grows ever more widespread. Fascism is on the rise. And we are rapidly approaching the tipping point of climate catastrophe. It's hard not to slip into despair, to feel overwhelmed by the magnitude of it all ... My prayers call me back to remembering there is a larger wholeness that breathes through all of Life. They help me believe that perhaps this turmoil—that seems so increasingly apocalyptic—can open the way for something better to emerge, if we meet it wisely.

Peril & Possibility

When most of us hear the word *apocalypse*, we think of catastrophe, cataclysm, and the end of existence. However, the archetype of apocalypse includes not only destruction, but revelation, and the opportunity for radical rebirth. These times are a portal calling us to discover the deeper Self that lies within each of us, and the possibilities for our collective evolution.

Traced back to the Greek root apocalypse means to uncover, to reveal what was hidden. Another layer of its definition, especially biblically, is a disclosure of knowledge. "Things are not getting worse, they are getting uncovered. We must hold each other tight and continue to pull back the veil," wrote author and activist adrienne maree brown, shortly after the 2016 US presidential election.[1] As the veil continues to be lifted, and more is revealed, the magnitude of intersecting perils becomes clear. But they are not new. Disinformation campaigns. Criminalization of the poor and the "other." Aggressive militarism. The unethical seizure of political power. Genocide. They are as old as empire, rooted in a consciousness of domination and toxic dualism. They reflect deep maladies within the soul of humanity—crises of meaning and maturity, manifesting now as devastating social and ecological upheaval.

A second Greek word is often paired with apocalypse: *apocatastasis*. It means restoration to an original wholeness. Mythologist Michael Meade describes the archetype of apocalypse and apocatastasis—destruction and renewal—as the collective rite of passage humanity now faces.[2] Meade has spent a lifetime studying the traditional stories of peoples the world over, and applying the wisdom of these stories to the issues of contemporary life and society. He explains that apocalyptic energies surface when an era is coming to an end and the previous worldview no longer holds people together. The purpose of this archetype is the progression from collapse to rebirth, inspiring an awakening of the soul that can help usher in the new era seeking to arise.

Indeed, further exploration of the meaning of apocalypse in religious contexts suggests that the "end of the world" it refers to is better understood as *the end of an age*. Given that we have been in an age rife with the structural, systemic, and political violences that professor bell hooks persistently named as imperialist white-supremacist capitalist patriarchy, that may not be such a bad thing. Nevertheless, empires don't die easy. They don't go down without a fight, and many painful casualties along the way. It could be that much of what we are witnessing now—including the horrific escalation of violence and repression—is because the structures of domination (and the consciousness that sustains them) are fighting for their lives, fighting to retain power. And they are fighting so hard precisely because they sense the turning tide.

At least that is my hope.

Meanwhile, in the midst of apocalypse, in the midst of so much suffering and destruction, how are we called to live? How do we hospice the dying world, while simultaneously midwifing the emerging one? How do we feel the very real desolation, and not be consumed by it? And how do we serve as agents of transformation in the alchemy of these times?

To do this requires healing. Healing our individual wounds, and healing the collective wounds of centuries of injustice. The two are inextricably joined. So many of our individual traumas are the result of systemic harms and inequity, and so many of those harms are rooted in the actions and decisions of people who are themselves traumatized.

Above all, what's needed is a healing of the wound of separation—our separation from our inner selves, and from each other, Nature, and the Divine (however we may conceive or understand that sacred essence). Healing does not mean an external cure or even, necessarily, the elimination of suffering. It's a restoration of inherent wholeness, an integration of what has been fractured in ourselves and in society. Through the process of healing we can turn our wounds into wisdom, and cultivate the spiritual maturity needed to enter a new way of living: a new relationship with one another and all of life. Only through the death of the worldview of division and domination can we birth a new reality. This is the opportunity offered to us through the upheaval.

The archetypal journey of death and rebirth is not only for the collective life of our abusive social constructs, it's an invitation for each of us individually, as well. If "apocalypse" means to reveal what has been hidden, perhaps that also includes the revelation of qualities within ourselves that are called forth to meet the chaos: insight, compassion, creativity, imagination, maturity, courage, perseverance, empathy, and so many others.

These gifts of the soul abide in us. They are the medicine that is needed for the world to make the transition from destruction to new life. The journey also requires we consider what within us may need to die so a greater wholeness can express. What are the patterns, beliefs, identities, and assumptions that are holding us back? Releasing them is also part of the healing process. Each of us has the capacity to contribute to the necessary transformation.

Surviving this passage will require a profound and paradigmatic transition—a progression from one way of understanding the world to another. It's like shifting the ideological tectonic plates that underlie the foundation of life in modern mechanistic societies: from domination to collaboration, commodification to reverence, division to oneness. This shift is not quick or simple, and traversing the territory between what-has-been and what-is-seeking-to-emerge can be an arduous task.

Alchemy of the In-Between

Poet and cultural theorist Gloria Anzaldúa wrote about the richly nuanced Nahuatl concept of *nepantla*. She referred to it as a state of in-between-ness, a liminal space where multiple realities simultaneously exist, and transformation can occur. Nepantla relates to both our individual journeys and our collective ones. Professor AnaLouise Keating, who worked closely with Anzaldúa, describes it this way: "During nepantla, our worldviews and self-identities are shattered. Nepantla is painful, messy, confusing, and chaotic; it signals unexpected, uncontrollable shifts, transitions, and changes. Nepantla hurts!!!! But nepantla is also a time of self-reflection, choice, and potential growth."[3] This is an apt description of the times we are in. From the unique perspective of the in-between, we are able to see beyond the limitations of the dominant society to imagine a world free of its constraints.

In the Abrahamic scriptures, the wilderness is another place of in-between-ness. Take the Exodus story about the Israelites' escape from bondage in Egypt: their journey through the wilderness lasted 40 years before they entered Canaan, or what was referred to as "the promised land." (It's important to recognize the complexities of intersecting stories, so while this is a narrative of liberation for the Israelites, it is also one of colonization for the peoples already inhabiting those lands, including the ancestors of today's Palestinians.) In the biblical allegory—the symbolic understanding of the story—the wilderness is a transitional place, a place of spiritual wrestling and formation. The physical terrain between Egypt and Canaan wasn't so vast that it took 40 years to cross. But the *spiritual evolution* necessary to move from a consciousness of bondage to a consciousness of liberation takes time. The people who emerged from the wilderness were not the ones who had entered it. The number 40, which signifies completion, is not intended here as a measure of chronological time, but as an indication of a period of trials in the transition from one way of being to another.

Wilderness times, like those of nepantla, are painful and difficult, and most of us want to get out of them as quickly as we can. Yet to shortchange the process is to pry open a cocoon prematurely because we want the butterfly. All we're going to find in there is goop, or a half-formed bug body with tiny useless wings. The question is not what do we need in order to get *out* of the wilderness, but rather, what do we need to *inhabit* the wilderness—for as long as it takes to complete our transition, our metamorphosis. You see, the wilderness is a *season* not a location. And like the healing of wounds, or the becoming of a butterfly, the wilderness journey is a process, not an event.

In a culture of "life hacks" and instant gratification, the idea of tarrying in the arduous in-between of spiritual wrestling may seem entirely unappealing. It's so tempting to want to bypass the wilderness and hurry on to the promised land. However, these experiences of formation and transformation are essential, lest we try to enter the new world with the same consciousness that created the old one.

Wildernesses are the crucible where we *become* the people who can live into new lands of promise and liberation. Without inner transformation, changes won in the outer world cannot be sustained. We may swap (for a time) who is on top and who is on the bottom of the social power structure, but unless the paradigm itself is shifted we will continue to reproduce the same dysfunctional dynamics.

To sustain ourselves through the rigors of the in-between we must be rooted in something deep enough to hold us steady, rich enough to provide nurture, and wise enough to guide us. I find that "something" in the collective power of community, and in the loving creative intelligence I call Spirit, especially as it is expressed through Nature. Maybe you find strength in your ancestors or cultural heritage, your movement comrades, or your religious faith. Whatever it is that connects us to a life-giving energy and a vision of possibility larger than ourselves must become part of our consistent practice.

Cycles of Death and Rebirth

Reflecting on these apocalyptic times, Valarie Kaur, founder of the Revolutionary Love Project, asks, "What if this is not the darkness of the tomb, but the darkness of the womb?"[4] The answer, of course, is it's both. Breakdowns and breakthroughs are happening at the same time. Endings and beginnings are simultaneous and overlapping; they require one another.

Nature itself is cyclical: the turning of seasons, the waxing and waning of the moon, the spiraling movement of day into night and into day again. Throughout history societies have come and gone, empires rise and fall. A number of traditional cultures describe a similar cycling of worlds, where the world-that-was comes to an end, and a new world gradually emerges. There's geological and archeological evidence to support this, but what interests me more than historical proofs is the spiritual wisdom that has been passed down through millennia, the teachings about how to face times of apocalyptic upheaval.

Stories of successive worlds are found in the lore of ancient Kemet, in Norse mythology, Toltec teachings, the yuga cycles in Hindu cosmology, and the prophecies of the Hopi Nation, among others. Flood narratives appear in dozens of cultures across almost every continent. Noah's Ark is one familiar version found in both the Hebrew Bible and the Holy Qur'an. In some of these accounts the destruction of worlds was precipitated by human beings losing sight of our essential belonging to the Earth, to one another and all creation. We ceased to live in harmony, acting in increasingly violent and extractive ways that ultimately led to our demise. Yet in these stories, there were those who remained in right relationship with larger Life: people who chose kinship, rather than othering and division, and who survived to seed the next world. That remembrance of belonging is the invitation—and the urgent necessity—of the times we inhabit.

We are not helpless bystanders at the mercy of apocalyptic changes; we have a role in the transformation. By actively engaging in healing the traumas and injustices of the past and present, and living in alignment with our soul's purpose, we help foster a shift in human consciousness so that the best possibilities for our collective life on this planet may be realized.

As the social and ecological collapse escalates around us, we are increasingly forced to live into the crucible of wilderness, the mystery of unknowing.

It's natural to be afraid. We can be afraid and still act—and even find fulfillment and beauty along the way. We must be willing to look at ourselves and our actions with honesty and humility, allowing the process to change us. We will feel our grief for the tremendous losses, extinctions, harms caused and experienced. We will grieve our places of complicity with those harms (whether they were intentional or not). Grief and suffering can bring us into our hearts, which is precisely where we need to be to create a world rooted in real care and reverence for the Sacred in its myriad expressions.

The current trajectory of endless consumption, individualism, and power-over dynamics is an accelerator toward death. What's called for is not going back to some idealized past, but moving forward, creating futures based on who we need to *become* and how we need to be with one another and Earth in order to survive. Crisis evokes creativity.

To birth a new world—to fight for it—we first have to imagine it possible. As author and innovator Sonya Renee Taylor notes, "The first practice of liberation is to think something new."[5] We can envision a different way of being together in and with the world. Not just focusing on what we fear or detest or resist (as mainstream media conditions us to do), but on the world we would love to see generations in the future. With every choice and act we are seeding that future.

What worlds are we seeding?
What would it look like to heal?
What would it feel like?

Dreaming about what might lie on the other side of apocalypse widens the threshold of possibility. We don't do this work of healing and awakening just for ourselves, but for our communities, ancestors, and descendants as an act of care. This is a collective undertaking, not an individual one. We are woven together with generations past and future, as well as with one another and every expression of existence—we are, none of us, alone.

Love is a radical form of resistance in an empire bent on dividing us from one another. It is the most powerful force of change imaginable. Together, we can alchemize the wounds of apocalyptic times into the medicine that brings a fractured world to wholeness.

Physician and author Rachel Naomi Remen sees healing as a worldview, a cosmology. From this perspective, the world is not "broken" and in need of fixing; rather there is a hidden wholeness in everything and everyone waiting to be revealed.[6]

Certain types of seeds can only germinate after a fire.[7] Their pods or cones remain sealed tight until the intense and sustained heat of the flames causes them to open. In the charred and smoldering remains of the landscape these precious gems give way to new life. Amazingly, it is the devastation that causes what had long been hidden to emerge. When it seems like all has been lost, only *then* does the moment of birth arrive. It's a powerful metaphor for this time of apocalypse. What hidden gems lie dormant within you, waiting for precisely the intensity of this season to take root and rise up?

The Choice Before Us

Following each epochal ending is a new beginning, with the next cycle of existence growing out of the remains of the old. This is the signature of Life evident everywhere in Nature. There is no doubt now that we are in a time of profound planetary upheaval, at an inflection point that will determine the future of life on Earth. The question, as I have come to understand it, is whether we will be collaborators with the transformation or casualties of the collapse.

Nature has offered us opportunities to come together as a global community in the face of pandemics and increasingly severe climate-related disasters. Still the addiction of industrialized capitalist nations to limitless growth and corporate profits keeps us on the path of destruction. Now, as I write this, we are facing the horrors of genocide and the threat of a third, and possibly nuclear, World War. Wisdom would lead us quickly to peaceful negotiation, yet the arrogant brutality of the dominant mindset reigns. What will it take for enough of us to wake up? How high must the consequences be for us to make the shift in both consciousness and behavior—away from the divisiveness of greed, enmity, and domination, and toward an embodied honoring of the sacred wholeness of Life?

These times can result in either rebirth or annihilation. We must discover a deeper purpose to guide us, and contribute what is ours to give toward the collective project of healing and transformation.

———— ◎ ————

REFLECTION PRACTICE

As you think about your own life, have you experienced "wilderness" times—times of transition when your self-identity or the shape of your world radically changed … times when you were in the difficult in-between of the unknown? It may even be that you are in one of those times now.

- *What did you learn from previous wilderness seasons?*
- *What was it you needed then, or what do you need now, to inhabit that in-between rather than trying to numb the discomfort or get out of it as quickly as possible?*
- *Is there something that needs to be released to allow what is seeking to emerge in you or in the world to come forward?*

I invite you to do some journaling to see what insights might surface.

*The meaning of our lives is not a static, singular thing,
but an emergent evolving process. By paying close attention
to the rhythm and heartbeat of our lives and by listening to
everything around us, meaning emerges.*

—Estelle Frankel

*Healing comes when the individual remembers his or her
identity—the purpose chosen in the world of ancestral
wisdom.... When we are connected—to our own purpose, to
the community around us, and to our spiritual wisdom—we
are able to live and act with authentic effectiveness.*

—Malidoma Somé

Do the work your soul must have.

—Katie Geneva Cannon

2
The Purpose of Our Living

AFTER CLASS ONE NIGHT, a student lingered to talk. She told me it
was her 73rd birthday. That evening's session had addressed
the spiritual quest for meaning and purpose in our lives, and
she confessed that she continued to move through the world in
search of hers. An accomplished, successful, and well-traveled
woman, she is a professional consultant with advanced degrees.
And still she longed to understand her soul's purpose. I hear
the same thing from people across the age spectrum—young
adults in their 20s and 30s, and those like my student, in what
is sometimes called "the third age" of our later years.

Having clarity on our purpose, and the larger purposes
of Life and human incarnation, offers both a compass and

a context. It can help locate us in the sacred pattern of the Whole. As we face increasingly widespread devastation, human awakening to our individual and collective purpose is an urgent matter for the survival of life on Earth. Times of crisis call us to our soul's intent, the reason we are alive *now*, at this crucial moment in the history of the world. What is it to be human on this planet? To be an Earthling: one species among many birthed of spirit and soil. How do we create a world that we know inside ourselves is just—not only for all humans, but for all of Life?

Purpose is not the same as goals or outcomes, or even vocation. Purpose is the larger quality of being our life is aimed toward; it's a direction not a destination. Goals and vocation are some of the tangible ways purpose is expressed; they should be aligned with our purpose, but they are the means rather than the ends. Purpose doesn't have an end. It's not something we complete and check off our list, but something larger than we are that we give ourselves to, something we live into day by day.

Purpose belongs to the soul rather than the ego. It is greater than our small self can manage, and thus we sometimes fear or resist its call. The "Divine idea" for our life is often beyond what we might ever imagine for ourselves—requiring faith, surrender, commitment, trust. Aligning with *that* is like swimming with the current, rather than against it.

When we lose sight of our soul's purpose, we can fall prey to the pseudo-purposes of a sick society, one that regards material success or the attainment of prestige and dominance as a worthy aim. But these are a shallow substitute and leave us empty. The void of this ceaseless hunger makes us vulnerable to addiction, consumerism, depression, anxiety, and hopelessness—endlessly searching for fulfillment. Studies show that having a sense of purpose is associated with feelings of well-being and hope, with life satisfaction, positive social relationships, self-esteem, and self-efficacy.[1] Purpose is beneficial to our physical health as well. It's correlated with longevity and positive indicators such as lower cholesterol levels, decreased inflammatory response, and a lower incidence of strokes, heart attacks, and dementia as we age.[2]

So how do we move toward an embodiment of this deeper sense of purpose? Describing the challenges of the 21st century, Detroit-based activist and philosopher Grace Lee Boggs often said, "These are the times to grow our souls."[3] We do this through facing the personal struggles inherent in human incarnation—loss and grief, conflict and reconciliation—but also through love, creativity, and wonder. And we grow our souls as we navigate the collective struggles of remaking an unjust society. The apocalyptic times we now inhabit must surely be among the greatest soul-growing opportunities ever offered on this precious planet.

I don't believe we are here, now, by accident, but rather that our souls chose to be present on Earth to contribute something in this pivotal season. Thus, part of our discernment is to ask what we are called to, and how we can live with purpose and meaning—not just *in spite of* the rising tide of calamities around us, but as our *response* to them—as the medicine for both ourselves and the world.

Our souls choose incarnation in order to grow in wisdom and maturity, and to participate in the evolution of the collective soul of humanity. This framework provides meaning and invites us to live into the best version of ourselves we can be. Just as we must exercise the body to build the strength and capacity of our physical muscles, we exercise the soul to build our "spiritual muscles." We even use that language: exercise patience, exercise faith, exercise compassion, and so forth. Physical muscles are developed through exertion against resistance—lifting weights against the resistance of gravity, for example, or pushing the body through the resistance of water as we swim. Surely in human life we encounter resistance everywhere. What if strengthening the capacities of our soul as we meet this resistance is one of the reasons we come?

Embodying Purpose

Renowned author, educator, preacher, and socially engaged mystic, Dr. Howard Thurman is among the most significant spiritual teachers in my own life. A few years back a quote from Thurman became a meme on social media. Even people who have no idea who he was recite this: "Don't ask yourself what the world needs. Ask yourself what makes you come alive, and go do that, because what the world needs is people who have come alive."[4] We come alive as we live in alignment with our soul's purpose, embodying and expressing our authentic self. It does not necessarily mean being happy all the time, or having material wealth, or being free from suffering and struggle. Indeed, the most vibrantly alive people push themselves beyond the bounds of ease and comfort, and take on challenges that require them to grow.

Discernment of purpose is a central theme in the seminary classes I teach, as well as my work in one-on-one counseling and mentoring. There are many approaches to this discernment, of course, but staying with Dr. Thurman, let's look at three questions he regularly asked people who were seeking clarity about their direction in life. I return to them again and again in my own spiritual practice, and share them with others. Each time, they yield new dimensions of understanding.[5]

Thurman begins the inquiry with this: "Who are you?" Then after a long pause, he asks, "Who are you . . . *really?*" It's something to meditate on, to walk with for a while before answering.

Out of that considered response, the next question he offers is, "What do you *want?*" The way he emphasizes *want* makes it clear this is not about a material or superficial desire, rather *what is the burning in your bones*, what is it that your soul must have. Sometimes he replaces the second question with "What are you *for?*" This might mean, what are you in favor of? Or, what is your usefulness? Both are fitting in a discernment of purpose.

Finally, after the seeker achieves some clarity on these reflections, the third question Thurman asks is, "How will you get it?"

So, first a question of identity, then one of values and calling, and lastly one of means and intent. He asked these a lot—in his writing, preaching, counseling. And in contemplating one's mortality, he also asked, "How have you lived your life in the knowledge of your truth?" (Which implies you must first have some clarity about your truth!)

In what is probably his best known book, *Jesus and the Disinherited*, Thurman introduces what he referred to as the "life's working paper" as a way to approach that exploration.[6] Each of us, he said, has a working paper that emerges from the totality of our personhood—our life experience, commitments, cultural and faith traditions, and our responses to the journey of living. In particular, the working paper comprises the values that guide our life, the questions we wrestle with, and how we respond to the compelling issues of our time. Thurman talks about the working paper of the prophet and teacher Jesus of Nazareth, and explores how it might serve as an invitation to our own. In other writing and speeches he talks about Life's working paper—the purposes of Life Itself—and how through careful examination we can find clues toward a fuller appreciation of what that might be.

As you contemplate your own purpose—and its expression in relation to your working paper—you may wish to ask:

> *What are your special gifts and capacities?*
> *What can you see from the vantage point of your experiences*
> * and social context?*
> *What are your core values?*
> *What is the urging in your heart for how to express and serve*
> * and make a difference?*

Recall the most challenging things you have faced, and notice what qualities or learnings you developed as a result. It is often our struggles and hardships that become the greatest source of our insight, and lead us to the unique contribution we offer the world. In Spirit nothing is wasted. Everything can be placed in service to purpose.

Brother Ishmael Tetteh, another of my most important spiritual teachers, is a Ghanaian mystic. He, too, suggests questions to guide our inquiry into purpose. Like Thurman, the first question he poses is one of identity: *What are the spiritual qualities that make you who you are?* You may be creative, insightful, healing, collaborative, nurturing, brave, disciplined, and so forth. He then asks, *"What is the impact that each of these qualities is seeking to bring into the world, as they express uniquely through you?"* Think of them as spiritual intelligences that contribute to the fulfillment of your soul's mission. So, for example, if "creative" is one of your qualities, how does the creative spirit in you seek to benefit others? It may be through performing music that lifts the heart, or coming up with innovative solutions to social problems.

Brother Tetteh's third question is one of vision. He asks, *"Through embodying these qualities and through their impacts, what is the world you want to see?"* It may be helpful to respond using a format like this: *I am a* ___, ___, ___ *person. My mission on Earth is (to)* _____. *For the realization of a world (that/of)* _____. (The mission and vision might each be a phrase, a sentence, or slightly longer.) Then imagine this world—see it, feel it, taste, hear, and smell it. Anchor it with your senses. As you go to sleep each night, and each morning as you awaken, dedicate yourself to your purpose. With each decision you make, you can ask if one choice or another would support or hinder your soul's purpose. The answer, then, can guide you. Allow your understanding of your purpose to grow within you, and reveal itself more fully over time.

Life's Unfolding Purpose

As you cultivate a climate of inward listening, realizations may come from unexpected places—including the world of Nature. One July morning I drove up into the Oakland hills to walk among the redwoods. Patches of sunlight shone through the dense branches onto the path before me. The still-cool air was fresh and fragrant; there were no other humans in sight. I was drawn to a circle of eleven trees with the decaying remains of a huge stump in the center—the Mother Tree. I sat on the ground beside her and listened.

This is legacy, I felt the trees telling me. Long after the Mother Tree was gone, the children that rose from her nourishing root stood tall and strong together, with their own tender progeny forming rings around their base. Even when the body of the Mother had crumbled completely back into the soil, her presence would live on through those generations, as she herself grew from the life force and bodies of those before her. Legacy is giving our life force to nurture a future we will never see. This insight places whatever we might understand as our individual purpose within the larger ongoing purpose of Life itself. Our contribution may seem small and inadequate, but it is part of a vast collective process that is unfolding across time.

So, how do we measure the impact of our lives? The answer I hear as I write this, is "in faithfulness." It's not the answer I expected. Yet, it makes so much sense. We may not ever know the number of people we touch, or what ripples of influence spread from each of those touches. But this isn't a numbers game; it's about our part in the evolution of Life—and being in integrity with that.

Our role may be to nurture one child who then goes on to change the world. Or to influence somebody who guides somebody who teaches somebody who touches somebody who changes the world. Or perhaps the world change comes not through outer actions at all, but through our being part of a small shift in collective consciousness. It may seem almost inconsequential at the fulcrum, however extended out across time, yields an entirely different trajectory. Think about it: If you are traveling in a straight line, or even a spiral, your destination will be a point further out on that trajectory. But if you alter the angle of your direction even a fraction and keep going forward from there, you'll end up in an entirely different place. The most minute changes can have a profound influence. When we tell the story about the person or event that "changed our life," we are pointing to this alteration in trajectory—sometimes dramatic, sometimes subtle, but in hindsight pivotal.

What does this mean for us now, in the collective, as we stand at the pivot point between annihilation and transformation? How many shifts in individual consciousness does it take to alter the trajectory of collective consciousness? And given the stakes, how can we do anything less than everything possible to contribute to this shift? Our purpose is what guides us in contributing whatever is ours to offer.

Whole-Souled Commitment

Our purpose is not simply a piece of information, it is an intentional practice we choose hour by hour, day by day. We are always practicing *something*, every moment of our lives. It's worthwhile to notice what we are practicing. Is it fear, worry, resentment, denial ... compassion, courage, equity ... separation or oneness? We can make our lives an embodiment of whatever we have discerned about our soul's intent. When we are aligned within ourselves, at our innermost core and with all that we are, it opens the channel for Life energy to rush in. Thurman talks about this as yielding "the nerve center of our consent." What have we said *yes* to at that inward center? To our wholeness? Our soul's purpose? Or to egoic desires and fears, society's definition of success, or even our own feelings of inadequacy? Making this whole-souled commitment to whatever it is—worthy or not, beneficial or not—unleashes the energy for its fulfillment.

Often we are a house divided in our own hearts and minds. We may want to dedicate ourselves to our highest ideals, but we also want comfort and safety. Or to be accepted. Perhaps we feel unworthy or incapable of rising to the demands of our soul's aspirations. We can observe the same dynamic on the larger scale. Most of the world's people yearn for peace—we pray for it, we sing about it, we preach and make speeches on it. As a nation we may say it's our intention, even our purpose, yet we persist in provoking and investing in war. We have not, as a collective, committed ourselves *fully* to peace and what it would require. We have not given it the "nerve center of our consent."

Since childhood, I have received nudges, insights, and messages from a wisdom beyond my own. Some people call this the inner teacher or guide. Some sense messages from their ancestors or from Nature. These insights may come to me in written form when I'm journaling, or as an intuitive knowing. It is this voiceless voice that guides my counseling sessions with clients and the retreats I facilitate. Over many years, I have learned to trust it and rely on its guidance. This message from 2015 talks about what it means to commit to our purpose. It is relevant to all of us in these times:

> To what do you commit the nerve center of your consent? This is more than just a mental exercise—it is a profoundly spiritual one. An alchemy. A combination to unlock your life and the fulfillment of Purpose. It is different than praying for something. Different even than surrender. It is your soul's assent—yea, more than that— your soul's unanimous irrevocable investment in Purpose. Are you willing to give your soul? Are you WILLING to give your SOUL? And if you have not yet given your soul to Purpose, what have you given it to? Where is it, daughter? Is it wandering? Or are parts of it waiting in the wings to be called forth? Waiting for a <u>demand worthy</u> of its fullness? It is time, daughter. It is time. Walk into your season. Make a worthy demand upon your soul, upon your life. One to which you can give your <u>whole</u> self. One that <u>requires</u> your full participation and resolve. One that uses ALL of you—your gifts <u>and</u> your frailties.[7]

The questions and invitations here are for everyone. And they are not to be taken lightly: To what have you given your soul's absolute consent, and are you willing to give it to sacred purpose? For much of my life I have been inching my way toward this commitment. It reminds me of going swimming as a kid, and when the water was soooo cold, I would ease my way into it little bit by little bit . . . getting used to it one tiny step at a time before at last taking the plunge. (Some folks said that made it harder, but I was never sufficiently convinced.)

Now, after so many years of inching, and with the pressing intensity of the calamities we face, my longing for the plunge is outweighing my trepidation.

It feels like a relief to live in greater and greater integrity with the demands of purpose I had resisted, to come ever closer to unanimous consent within myself. The energetic force available within this is palpable. My practice now is to evoke it daily, to consciously move into it and engage it to amplify the collective healing work I feel called to. It's an intentional discipline, with many lapses throughout the day—or even for days or weeks at a time. (This is why we call it *practice*!) Yet returning again and again to remembrance, these spiritual muscles gain strength.

Nelson Mandela counseled, "There is no passion to be found in playing small—in settling for a life that is less than the one you are capable of living." Spiritual teacher and healer Malidoma Somé adds: "In an indigenous perspective we see ourselves as an offering, just as everything we see is a gift to us. It is not healing or constructive to see ourselves as just the recipient of beauty. We must also be a gift to that beauty."[8] We can make our lives an offering to Life: stretch beyond the margins of our comfort zone, and be willing to put everything we are and have been through in service to the urgent calling of these times. Nothing and no one is inconsequential in an interdependent world on the brink of catastrophe.

Making this offering, this commitment, leads us into another kind of portal, one where we are birthed into a life of greater meaning. It can feel both exhilarating and terrifying. In her poignant "Letter to a Young Activist During Troubled Times," psychoanalyst and author Clarissa Pinkola Estés offers encouragement. She writes,

> *Mis estimados.* Do not lose heart. We were made for these times.... Ours is not the task of fixing the entire world all at once, but of stretching out to mend the part

of the world that is within our reach. . . . It is not given to us to know which acts or by whom, will cause the critical mass to tip toward an enduring good. . . . [T]here can be no despair when you remember why you came to Earth, who you serve, and who sent you here."[9]

---◎---

REFLECTION PRACTICE

This chapter contains several approaches for discerning your soul's purpose. Start with the one you are most drawn to, and take some time with it to see what emerges. Remember this is a process that evolves. Continue to live into these questions, revisit them, and allow the layers of clarity to come as they are ready. When you're facing a decision, ask if one choice or another would support or hinder your purpose. Allow your purpose to become a compass to guide your life toward greater meaning. What would it require for you to "commit the nerve center of your consent" to your deeper purpose?

Initiation is an ordeal, a tempering induced by heat and pressure. Heat we have and pressure aplenty. The circumstances of our lives and in the surrounding world, are the initiatory thresholds compelling us to change.

—Francis Weller

Feel into the mystery, not knowing what you may touch.... In the midst of an initiation, how you see life is tested and if you are open, it will transform you. Going forward, you'll see the world in a different way.

—Zenju Earthlyn Manuel

Only when you emerge from the dead with soul intact can you honor the visions you dreamed in the depths. In the deep fecund cave of gestation lies not only the source of your woundedness and your passion, but also the promise of inner knowledge, healing, and spiritual rebirth (the hidden treasures), waiting for you to bear them to the surface.

—Gloria Anzaldúa

3
Thresholds of Initiation

AS APOCALYPTIC UPHEAVALS CAUSE systems to collapse, and the familiar world is torn away, we are drawn into a portal of individual and collective initiation. A transformational rite of passage, initiation reshapes our sense of self. It's a threshold between one reality or way of being and another. Not unlike the wilderness journey we explored in the first chapter, initiation encompasses the mysteries of life, death, and renewal. Through the process we are stripped until nothing but our most essential core remains. We die to the narrow concerns of egoic mind, and discover our soul's purpose in the community of Life.

The current initiations are happening to the individual and the world at the same time. The particular personal experience each of us is having, within the national and international turmoil, within the global pandemics, within the climate crisis and the turning of the age, reminds me of nesting folk dolls, every doll—every turmoil—held within the next larger sized one. Yet there is hope in this. When superficial concerns are torn away, the deep Self that lies in each of us may be revealed. And as more of us emerge from the cauldron of initiation and live into our gifts and purpose, a widespread awakening is kindled. Each individual soul is part of the soul of the world; each awakening, each transformation, contributes to the awakening whole.

Seeing the multiple crises we face in the global community as part of a larger collective initiation invites us to engage them with sacred intent, and provides a context through which to find meaning and direction. The same is possible for our individual traumas. The archetype of initiation can help orient us as we move through trauma toward greater self-understanding, maturity, and connection. Trauma disrupts relationships—with self, body, others, Earth, and all beings. Through initiation we have the opportunity to reclaim our intimacy with the Divine and our inherent belonging to the unfolding cosmos.

The Path of Initiation

Initiatory practices exist in many faiths and cultural traditions. Echoes of these rites even persist in secular modernity. For example, weddings signify the end of single life and begin a new identity as a married person. Childbirth and adoption mark the entry into parenthood. Graduation ceremonies after years of training in medicine, law, or teaching herald admission into professional service in those disciplines. In modern society, however, the spiritual significance and rigors of initiation are often absent, and our maturity as a culture has suffered as a result.

True initiations demand something extraordinary of us, and leave us profoundly changed.

We can best begin to learn about the deeper spiritual dimensions of initiation by consulting the cultures practicing it consistently for millennia. In Burkina Faso, West Africa, Malidoma Somé was an elder of the Dagara people. His ancestors called him to be a bridge, bringing the teachings of the Dagara to Europe and the US. Through this, they hoped to awaken the people in these imperialist nations who had forgotten their own ancestral wisdom, and thus further the transformation so urgently needed in today's world. Somé explained, "Finding one's purpose is the primary goal of initiation. It also teaches responsibility toward community, village, and culture." We all enter life "with a gift that we must give to the world," he said. "We must undergo initiation to discover what our gift is and how to share it."[1]

While Somé does not advocate people in the West undergo the type of initiation that takes place in African and other Indigenous cultures—since that is not their cultural tradition—he does suggest that some aspects of initiation would help western societies come into a greater maturity, and better understand their place within the circle of Life. Such awakening is needed to move through all that confronts us in this era of violent upheaval.

In his autobiographical book *Of Water and the Spirit*, Somé shares glimpses of his own initiation, a grueling six-week trial as part of a group of young men shepherded by a small circle of elders.[2] Pushing him beyond the limits of rational mind, beyond the endurance of his physical body, and into the depths and heights of emotion, it released something in him previously unknown. He became aware of a multidimensionality, a magic and a wisdom that is everywhere, in everything. And he felt his inseparable oneness with it all.

He describes three stages within the initiatory process.[3] The first is a departure from or disruption of one's ordinary life. In Somé's case, he and his fellow initiates left the village, entering the bush and the altered reality of the spiritual quest. The second stage is characterized by a period of ordeals, trials, and uncertainty. These may be frightening, painful, disorienting, or even life-threatening. They forced Somé into a liminal place of expanded perception, and revelation. Finally comes the third stage of return or homecoming—not returning to what was, but being welcomed into the community in one's new identity. Among the Dagara, the entire village joins in ritual celebration, affirming the initiates in their emergent status. Mentors and elders provide ongoing guidance to support the healthy integration of the ordeal, as the initiates begin to live into the purpose that has been opened to them.

Not everyone survives initiation. Actually, in a sense, no one survives initiation as who they once were. There is either transformation within the life or transformation out of it. This is true for the individual initiate, and true for the planetary initiations we now face. We cannot survive this collective ordeal as who we have been.

Acknowledging the trials we are undergoing collectively on planet Earth as an initiation confers a sense of spiritual significance, and offers us a fresh perspective on how to navigate these times. As we confront ecological crises, pandemics, and societal collapse, regarding these events from the standpoint of initiation can shift our experience from one of helplessness in the face of global calamities, to one of purposeful engagement, pushing us to release outworn ways of being and step into our collective wisdom. Similarly, we can see the trials and traumas of our individual lives through the lens of initiation as a way to find meaning and resolution.

This is not to suggest that trauma in and of itself is initiatory, but that the archetypal framework of initiation can offer a path toward integration. The word *integrate* means to bring together two or more things to create a unified whole. It is through bringing together the parts of ourselves or our communities fractured by trauma that we promote healing. This is a process of honoring our wounds, our strengths, our stories, and our learnings, as we become the people that can hold them all from a place of empowerment. Integration is part of completing an initiation and living into its gifts.

Traumatic "Initiations" of the Modern World

Trauma can be understood as the lingering impact of experiencing a physical, emotional, spiritual, or psychological harm so distressing it overwhelms our ability to cope.[4] The etymology of the word is Greek, meaning a wound, a hurt, or a defeat. Dr. Gabor Maté is an expert in trauma and addiction. His own traumatic experience as a young Jewish child in Budapest during the Nazi occupation of World War II later led him to specialize in working with trauma survivors. "Trauma is not what happened to you," he explains, "it's what happens inside you as a result of what happened to you. So the sexual abuse or the neglect or the war tragedy is not the trauma—that's the traumatic event that induces the trauma—the trauma is the wound that you sustain."[5] Trauma is the *response* to a highly stressful or painful event, or series of events, but not everybody who experiences those events will develop trauma. A traumatic response is more likely to result when we feel unsupported and alone in the face of the experience, when our sense of safety, belonging, and dignity is ruptured. Somatics practitioner and innovator Staci Hanes identifies these elements—safety, belonging, and dignity—as the interdependent core necessities for human well-being.[6]

In the absence of an organized initiatory practice, our lives may become full of haphazard and fragmented initiatory experiences that never come to an integrative conclusion. Things like illness, depression, abuse, war, tragic loss or injury, can all become traumatic pathways of initiation. They may even follow the same three-part pattern described by Somé in the account of his own initiation. First, traumatic events disrupt the normal flow of our lives, then throw us into a period of uncertainty and tribulation. Far too often, however, we are missing the final step of return and welcome. Without that, and without support to integrate what we have undergone, we might be left with nothing but the anguish of trauma. Resolution is never reached.

These erratic "initiations" in contemporary western societies, Malidoma Somé observes, "happen to just about everyone in this culture. Homecoming requires recognition and acknowledgment that the person has survived. Most people don't get this," he points out, "which causes them to go back into the ordeal.... What people need is someone willing to create a space for them in which they can be seen, honored, and praised for what they have been through. The psyche knows when a homecoming is genuine."[7]

While community embrace is essential to bring closure to an initiatory experience, such welcome alone is not sufficient. We also need guidance and support to process what we have been through, to move forward into a greater wholeness.

In places where initiation is part of the fabric of life, the initiate is supported by a spiritual "container" of culture, guiding elders, and the encouragement of community. In modern settings where the importance of spiritual elders is not recognized, it may be a therapist, a pastor or imam, or even a 12-step program sponsor who supports the resolution and integration of an initiatory passage. In 12-step meetings like Alcoholics Anonymous, as each person speaks, they introduce themselves, and the group responds in one voice, welcoming them by name.[8] I cannot help but see a connection here. Does this communal welcome into the fellowship of recovery signal to the psyche that the "initiation" of addiction and its ordeals can now become the work of integration? The process may not be so simple and decisive. It takes commitment and mentorship to "work the steps" of recovery, break free from old patterns, and find greater meaning for our lives.

Unfortunately, many therapists and clergy lack the framework to engage trauma in this context, or haven't integrated their own initiatory experiences. It's nearly impossible to guide others through territory one has not traversed. This is not to say the guide has to have gone through the same trauma, rather that they have to have done enough healing in themselves to integrate whatever their own trials have been.

Survivors of the carceral system, domestic violence, or childhood abuse may also be left without adequate support for healing and integration. Even as we seek to transform the social structures and conditions that lead to such harms, we must attend to the well-being of impacted individuals and communities. Given the prevalence of trauma—of all types and degrees—perhaps we can help foster healthy integration of these ordeals by approaching them as initiations. What might open up if we turned to ritual to anchor and affirm their conclusion, encourage embodiment of the learnings, and support moving forward in a good way? If the intent of the initiation archetype is about dying to the small self, developing spiritual maturity, and living into our purpose, what does this signify for us? What needs to die within us, and what does that death allow to emerge in us and in the world? We might, for example, need to die to the sense of being a victim or feeling unworthy, and open ourselves to being born into our full agency, able to live into our soul's great gift, the unique genius that lies within.

One innovative organization taking this approach is Ritual4Return (R4R), a twelve-week rites of passage program for formerly incarcerated people. It utilizes an initiation framework to help participants transition from the imposed identity of "convict" or "prisoner" and re-enter the world as their empowered authentic selves. The program incorporates mindfulness, self-reflection, drumming, theatrical and expressive arts, along with the support of facilitators and co-initiate peers. The R4R website explains: "It is a demanding journey, pushing people intellectually, physically, emotionally, and spiritually as they define and then cross the thresholds that mark the transition from bondage to freedom."[9] The program ends with a community rites of passage ceremony attended by loved ones who witness, affirm, and welcome the participants into a fresh chapter of their lives. Deeply healing for all involved, this ritual marks the conclusion of the long initiatory trek through trauma, abuse, and incarceration.

It isn't always so straightforward. Yes, healing the wounds of trauma can bring liberation, but not everybody reaches that place. What is it that causes some people to heal, move on in life, and even thrive in the wake of trauma, while others remain devastated by its lingering impacts? How do we increase the likelihood of integration and resolution? Through examining a phenomenon known as post-traumatic growth, we can find useful clues and compelling parallels to the initiatory process.

Post-Traumatic Growth

You may be familiar with post-traumatic stress disorder (PTSD), where intense, disturbing thoughts and feelings related to a traumatizing experience persist long after the traumatic events have ended. Less commonly talked about is post-traumatic growth, when positive transformation takes place through healing trauma.[10] People experiencing post-traumatic growth report a greater appreciation for life, more compassion and empathy for others, and a recognition of their own personal strength. They may undergo a shift in priorities that leads them to explore new possibilities, focus more on spirituality, and cultivate a sense of meaning and purpose. (You'll notice similarities here to the fruits of initiation.) These things don't arise automatically, but come as the result of a dedicated journey of learning, reflection, and integration.

Post-traumatic growth is both a process and an outcome. It can, and often does, co-exist with PTSD, yet although we may still have flashbacks and other aftereffects of trauma, we are able to work with them in a different way. As with initiation, the goal is not to somehow return to who we were before the ordeal, but to progress into a deeper relationship with Life and Self.

Several factors promote post-traumatic growth. First, learning about the effects of trauma to encourage self-awareness and self-compassion, realizing that it's possible to emerge from the trauma more whole and empowered. Then, having supportive relationships—trusted people to talk with about the trauma and its impacts—offers a crucial sense of connection. This, and other forms of reflection like journaling, meditation, poetry or art, can promote insight and release. In addition, connection with Spirit and Nature—positive forces greater than the trauma—can be profoundly healing.

Key to post-traumatic growth is the meaning we ascribe to the experience of trauma, and our ability to (re)define our life narrative in a way that creates some sense of purpose out of the ordeal. There are people who believe that everything happens for a reason. I'm not sure about that, but I do believe that nothing happens without the potential for meaning. Many survivors find meaning in being of service, benefitting others in some way, perhaps related to what they went through. Survivors of gun violence, for example, may serve as counselors to others affected by this trauma, or they might choose to work for gun control legislation, or to change the underlying social conditions that lead to violence.

This connection with meaning, purpose, and service echoes the intention of initiation as described by Somé. He explains that the maturity developed through initiation "must be understood as the awakening of one's gifts and the investment of self for a good that is greater than self."[11] In working through any pain or difficulty, we might ask:

What can I learn here?
What is seeking to be healed in me, in the situation, and in the world?
What is in this for me to understand, cultivate, contribute, or transform that would redeem it into a blessing?
Who do I want to be on the other side of this, and what choices and changes can I make now to become that person?

Finding Meaning through Reframing the Narrative

Michael Meade uses traditional myths and folk stories as archetypal maps to supply new context to the traumas we endure. Like his longtime friend and collaborator Malidoma Somé, he suggests that unhealed trauma can be seen as an unfinished story of initiation, calling for completion. Meade recounts a severely traumatizing time in his own life. Drafted into the US war on Vietnam, he refused to fight and eventually ended up in solitary confinement in a military prison. For months he remained on a hunger strike in protest, his weight dropping from 150 to 87 pounds. He was beaten and berated, coming close to death before finally being released.

For many years afterward, Meade recalls,

> the battle continued unabated within me as I tried to adapt to regular life.... I was in a post-traumatic condition; but I was also in an unfinished story that only left me feeling a stranger in a strange land. Studying the old ideas of rites of passage and initiatory practices helped me make sense of what could feel hopelessly traumatic and senselessly painful. The three-fold pattern of separation, ordeal, and return gave a narrative shape and meaning to otherwise overwhelming and confusing events. I began to re-work my own experiences with the sense that they were part of a lifelong initiation and continuing process of self-revelation.[12]

This perspective became foundational to Meade's later work—some in partnership with Somé—with men's groups, veterans, and gang-involved youth, guiding participants in creating their own rituals for collective healing, and finding purpose through the initiatory traumas in their lives.

Addressing trauma through a framework of initiation invites us into to the realm of the spiritual, and provides an array of healing modalities that may be a valuable adjunct to conventional therapies. Standard medical and psychothera-peutic treatments can be life-saving, but without attention to the spiritual component, there are times when the root of an injury persists. To address the wounds of the soul, we can reach beyond the level of the intellect, to activate the symbolic language of archetype and ritual. We can call on the support of ancestors, Nature, and the energies of the Divine to help release what is holding us back, to reveal what we need to know, and to aid us in moving through the initiatory portal toward integration and purpose.

When we see our traumas as an initiation, it opens the way for a greater sense of agency and purpose. Traumatic events are something beyond our control that happen to us—that shock, disrupt, victimize. And initiation is a sacred process we can engage with intention to come more fully into wholeness. The archetypal framework of initiation provides a "container" that is missing for many of us in the face of trauma. Approaching our experience as part of an initiatory process can begin to help restore the feeling of dignity, belonging, and safety ruptured by traumatic events.

Collective Trauma, Collective Initiation, Collective Healing

Woven throughout the experience of individual trauma is collective, historical, and ancestral trauma, as well as the ongoing trauma of societal oppression.[13] None of these are separate from the other, and all must be addressed on the path toward healing. As we move from microcosm to macrocosm—individual to collective—and seek to confront the historical harms that have shaped our social structures and attitudes, it's possible we can gain new perspectives by approaching these traumas, too, through the lens of initiation and the archetypal pattern of death–transformation–rebirth.

The US was forged out of trauma, and is maintained by trauma. The land is steeped in trauma. Trauma lives in the bones and blood of every human body in this nation. I write about the US because this is the country I live in and know best. And because it is the source of so much global harm. But trauma is present for any land and people touched by the violence of settler colonialism, genocide, or enslavement.

The violences that shaped this nation are staggering. And the violences we continue to commit here and around the world amplify this legacy of harm every single day. You see, the past is never completely in the past, it lives in us moment by moment, and we will keep repeating these historic abuses until we engage in a reparative and transformational process to heal them. As with the individual, unaddressed collective harms are embodied as generational cycles of trauma; integrated and healed, they can become wisdom and a new future is made possible.

The suppression and outright denial of US history championed by what has been called the "anti-woke" movement is a dangerous example of how this operates. Banning books and rewriting school curricula erases parts of our common story necessary to our integrity and maturity as a society. In denying the wounds of our historical abuses we also deny the strengths and learnings that can arise from them. Unhealed trauma blunts empathy, disinhibits cruelty, and deadens the heart. It can numb us to the ongoing horrors of war, genocide, or ecological catastrophe, and lead to the devastating consequences of inaction.

The multiple crises of the current age require us to contend with this toxic legacy, whatever our particular location within it might be. Those who enact harm and those persecuted by it are both wounded, and the line between the categories of oppressor and oppressed is not absolute. We may be subjugated based on our identity in one or more area—such as ethnicity or economic status—but part of the subjugating group in another, maybe through gender or sexual orientation. Historically, too, a group that has been the victim of systematic brutality may then turn and perpetrate egregious harm on another population.

Ending this pattern requires we reckon with all of it, not allowing our traumas to be weaponized against one another to create further harm and division.

The wholeness of the world requires that each of us be made whole. We feel one another—consciously or not. We breathe one another's air and sense one another's suffering. Our individual nervous systems are plugged into a collective nervous system; our soul is part of a collective soul. This connection is not only a prescription for pain, however; it is a resource for healing. Each individual awakening impacts us all. Every act of radical beauty, generosity, courage, or kinship amplifies those qualities in the collective heart and shifts the tide toward liberation. The traumatic imprint is not indelible. We can heal. We can transform. We can get free.

As a collective initiation, the coronavirus pandemic and extended isolation, escalating climate crisis, political upheaval, and rising threat of global war have thrust us into disruption, ordeals, and uncertainty. To survive this crucible, we must heed the guidance of spiritual elders and the wisdom of Nature. We must awaken the soul of humanity to its sacred purpose and remember our oneness with all of Life. Just as the "return" stage of personal initiation is not a return to the previous state, neither is the world's in this global rite of passage. We can use the disruption as an opportunity to transform. We can consciously choose *not* to go "back to normal," when normal was an entrenched system of oppression that benefitted the few to the detriment of the many and of the Earth.

In her April 2020 essay, "The Pandemic Is a Portal," Arundhati Roy writes,

> Whatever it is, coronavirus has made the mighty kneel and brought the world to a halt like nothing else could. . . . And in the midst of this terrible despair, it

offers us a chance to rethink the doomsday machine we have built for ourselves. Nothing could be worse than a return to normality. Historically, pandemics have forced humans to break with the past and imagine their world anew. This one is no different. It is a portal, a gateway between one world and the next. We can choose to walk through it, dragging the carcasses of our prejudice and hatred, our avarice, our data banks and dead ideas, our dead rivers and smoky skies behind us. Or we can walk through lightly, with little luggage, ready to imagine another world. And ready to fight for it.[14]

Several years later, it would seem that we squandered the invitation offered to us through the pandemic. Mainstream society clings stubbornly to a mindset that is rapidly leading to our demise. Governments are increasingly out of step with the people they are supposed to represent, and we see greater levels of repression and extremism as dominant forces seek to retain power.

Yet *at the same time*, there are more and more people rising in solidarity to demand a change in direction, more people quietly creating alternative systems for collective flourishing, more seeking to live in harmony with one another, Earth, and cosmos. Just as the intention of initiation in the individual is to call forth the soul gifts within them to serve the common good, so can this collective initiation call forth the genius in the soul of humanity.

At one of the online healing retreats I facilitated during covid, I invited participants to consider a couple of the questions offered in the above section on post-traumatic growth: *who do you want to be on the other side of this, and what choices and changes can you make now to become that person?* The question extends beyond covid to the multiple crises before us, and from the personal to the collective. It's an invitation for all of us—who do we want to be as a nation, as a world community, as part of the family of Earth? What future might that create, and what enables us to live into those ideals? We have to step outside the parameters defined by empire and into the creative imagination of our relationship with all of Life. This is the sacred community to which we must return to bring the cycle of initiation to its conclusion.

———————— ◎ ————————

REFLECTION PRACTICE

How can looking at your own traumatic experiences and the global crises we face through the lens of initiation shift the way we understand and engage them? I encourage you to do some journaling to reflect on the questions offered in this chapter—from both a personal and a planetary perspective—to meditate on your responses, and talk about them with others:

- *What can I (we) learn here?*
- *What is seeking to be healed in me (us), in the situation, and in the world?*
- *What is in this for me (us) to understand, cultivate, contribute, or transform that would redeem it into a blessing?*
- *Who do I (we) want to be on the other side of this, and what choices and changes can I (we) make now to become that person / nation / world?*
- *What future might that create, and what is required to live into those ideals?*

PART TWO

Restoring Wholeness

Our inner healing is intimately tied to the healing of the world.

There is a Sacred Wound, which reframes life's cruelties and betrayals, both physical and psychological, in such a fashion we come to see them as gateways to deeper understanding, greater vulnerability, and empathy.

—Jean Houston

Sometimes we're fractured by the choices we make; sometimes we're shattered by things we never would have chosen. But our brokenness is also the source of our common humanity, the basis of our shared search for comfort, meaning, and healing. Our shared vulnerability and imperfection nurtures and sustains our capacity for compassion.

—Bryan Stevenson

Healing isn't linear, and it doesn't happen in isolation.
—Michelle Cassandra Johnson

4

The Medicine in Our Wounds

ILLNESS HAS BEEN MY OWN protracted initiation, and the source of my most profound growth. It has helped lead me toward my soul's purpose. For more than 50 years my life has been shaped—in greater or lesser degrees—by Crohn's Disease, an autoimmune disorder that primarily affects the digestive system. In autoimmune diseases the body attacks its own tissues, seeking to destroy them the way it would a viral or bacterial invader. A chronic incurable condition with an uneven course of flare-ups and remissions, Crohn's affects each person differently: for some it's relatively mild, for others life-threatening. My illness has been on the severe end of the spectrum.

My belly is crossed with surgical scars. Seven times it has been flayed open at the midline, leaving an uneven puckered trail. Under and around the physical scars is the emotional wounding that comes with chronic and disabling illness: the shame of disfigurement, of feeling damaged and undesirable ... the loneliness of isolation and unbelonging ... the dread of each further progression of disease ... the grief of not being able to live without constraint. These are the invisible scars that wind through every relationship, interaction, and decision, and that over time shape a life. I am who I am because of these scars, this illness, this history.

Five times I have come close to the threshold of death. Five times I have made the choice to turn around and live a while longer. And each time it has been a choice. A difficult choice. I have often longed for that sweet return to an imagined spiritual home. But I believe we come into this life, in whatever form and condition we inhabit, for a purpose. I knew I wasn't done with mine, so I made the decision to stay, to take whatever the next course of medication or surgery might be; each time acclimating to a new compromised baseline.

Periods of illness pulled me into a liminal space, outside of time and the activities of the world ... forced me to be still, and learn to listen. Illness has been my teacher and my tormenter, my shepherd and spiritual guide. It was illness that pushed me into daily spiritual practice as a matter of survival. Illness that led me to study an array of healing traditions. It was illness that deepened my humanity, that taught me patience, resilience, and the power in surrender. And over time, illness has helped me fall in love with life—perhaps in part *because* of its tenuousness. I have grown to savor the minute sensory details of Nature, the precious gift of relationships, the exquisite ordinary beauty that is everywhere. The miracle of everything.

Years ago, I asked myself if I could live my life over without Crohn's Disease, would I? The answer surprised me: *I would choose*

Crohn's. As brutal as this journey has been, I'm not sure I would like who I might have become without it—probably more driven, less compassionate and intuitive, and lacking a depth of spiritual maturity. The realization that I would choose illness again was liberating. No longer was I the victim of some great misfortune, or guilty of a personal failure for "manifesting" adversity. That is not to say my humanness doesn't sometimes wish my body was healthy, that I don't long for what a healthy body would make possible. But I don't set up camp there; it is not my habitation.

I lament the rising tide of limitation and malaise, and the isolation it causes, but there are ways that illness, and the suffering of illness, is a point of connection. An unspoken common ground with the vast suffering of people everywhere, a belonging to the "place" of humanness. My work in the world, and the work of my heart, encompasses both ministry—counseling, healing, tending, teaching—and an activist commitment to social justice and transformation. I would not be as effective at either without this personal understanding of suffering. So I find the gifts, even in the pain.

Perhaps you have also endured the fires of illness. Or maybe your struggle has been addiction, a dramatic loss, or a history of abuse. I am not trying to romanticize or valorize suffering, but to encourage meeting *whatever* we face with sacred intent, so we may come to know its wisdom.

The trials in our life can force us into unplumbed dimensions of our being, pushing us to develop qualities and abilities that would elseways not have been possible. Challenges and tribulation call forth something more from us than business-as-usual, as we rise to meet them. Not that we require suffering for redemption—as some theologies assert—but rather that the experience of suffering may *itself* be redeemed through our choice to use it to reveal a greater good: to grow in spiritual maturity, to motivate activism for justice, to stimulate a creative solution, to feel our kinship with others, to cultivate compassion.

Changing Poison into Medicine

Howard Thurman talks about suffering as a discipline of the spirit. Many of us may be used to thinking of spiritual disciplines as practices we intentionally undertake to develop our inner life—meditation, prayer, the study of sacred texts, and the like. But suffering? Thurman describes the aim of spiritual disciplines as removing the barriers to what he calls our "inner altar," our unmediated communion with the Divine. Suffering and pain, he explains, can gather our energies in a single-pointed focus as competing demands fall away, and thus may become a doorway into deeper intimacy with Spirit and reflection on the meaning of existence.

In his meditation "Pain Has a Ministry" Thurman identifies the purpose of life as soul-making: "the development of . . . a sensitiveness, a depth of being, which would put [us] in the fullest possession of all [our] powers; in other words, make [us] whole."[1] He goes on to say, "The pain of life may teach us to understand life and, in our understanding of life, to love life. To love life truly is to be whole in all one's parts; and to be whole in all one's parts is to be free and unafraid."[2] There is a liberation that can arise from the crucible of suffering. When we realize that all the fire's raging, all the blustering of the storm can only "touch the outer walls of [our] dwelling place"[3] and that the inner sanctum of our soul remains forever unscathed, we are set free.

Suffering provides a humbling and unrelenting reminder of our humanness. However, by approaching suffering with the discipline of spiritual intention, it becomes possible to reach beyond the limitations of our humanness—if even for a moment—to touch the transcendent. In his book *Disciplines of the Spirit*, Thurman observes that people may be "profoundly changed by their suffering. Into their faces [may] come a subtle radiance and a settled serenity; into their relationships a vital generosity that opens the sealed doors of the heart in all who are encountered along the way. Such people," he says, "look out upon life with quiet eyes. Openings are made in a life by suffering that are not made any other way. Serious questions are raised and primary answers come forth. Insights are reached concerning aspects of life that were hidden and obscure before the assault."[4] Thurman acknowledges that not everyone responds to suffering this way. Some people become embittered and close in upon themselves; still others seek ways to numb or avoid the pain.

The meaning we attribute to something, the explanatory story we tell ourselves about it—whether about events, experiences, people, or nations—shapes how we respond to them. It shapes how we approach our personal tribulations, and how we engage these times of collective crisis and upheaval. Austrian psychiatrist and survivor of the Nazi death camps, Viktor Frankl, has noted, "Despair is suffering without meaning."[5] He describes an inverse relationship where increasing meaning causes a decrease in despair, and notes that while we may not be able to change the conditions of our affliction, we *can* address meaning and thereby shift the context and experience of suffering. This has certainly been the case for me on my own long walk with illness. And although the reframing took years to reach and my practice of it remains far from perfect, engaging suffering as a spiritual discipline, and recognizing the gifts of growth it has brought, has provided meaning and the capacity to not only endure but to flourish.

There is one interpretation sometimes assigned to suffering and adversity, however, that I particularly want to challenge. In certain religious contexts suffering may be seen as a sign of spiritual shortcoming, lack of faith, or punishment for God's disfavor. I regard this as theological malpractice. Suffering is a natural part of human life. Heaping guilt, shame, and blame on top of it only increases the burden of pain and hinders its transformative potential.

In Nichiren Buddhism there's a teaching about "changing poison into medicine." It affirms that nothing and no one is beyond the possibility of redemption. Suffering can be turned into wisdom, and even happiness. They say the "process of changing poison into medicine begins when we approach difficult experiences as an opportunity to reflect on ourselves and to strengthen and develop our courage and compassion."[6] However, if we "respond to challenging circumstances in negative and destructive ways, the original 'poison' is not transformed but remains poison."[7] Value arises from the commitment to self-knowledge and growth.

This meaning-making and medicine-turning is something I do in my counseling work and with the people I mentor. I think of it as a kind of spiritual *aikido*. Established by Japanese martial artist Morihei Ueshiba in the early 20th century, aikido is a synthesis of his martial studies, philosophy, and religious beliefs.[8] The word "aikido" is often translated as "the way of harmonizing energy." The intent of this practice is not to harm the opponent, but to blend with their energy, redirecting the force of the attack rather than fighting it head-on.[9] The victory in aikido, according to Ueshiba, is over *oneself*, rather than over any external entity.

I find it a helpful metaphor for healing and spiritual practice, where instead of meeting an affliction with the force of opposition, we yield to it in order to redirect it in a beneficial way. This shifts our relationship with the "opponents" of suffering and adversity, restores agency, and opens up an array of possible responses . . . and gifts. In my own life, for example, after many rounds of resisting and being knocked out by Crohn's Disease, I learned to listen to it, to yield to its demands for me to be still, and then used that stillness to nurture my spiritual life.

Malidoma Somé taught that adversity calls forth genius. It invites us to draw on inmost resources of the soul and develop qualities within ourselves that might otherwise go unrealized. Echoing his discussion of initiation, he said the greatest blessing often sits behind that which we think is an ordeal, and we must constantly push ourselves to the edge—beyond our comfort zone.[10] Years ago I came across a meme that makes the point. A chalkboard drawing of a small circle contained the words "Your Comfort Zone." Outside the circle were the words "Where the Magic Happens."

Perhaps our personal passages through the terrain of suffering prepare us for the collective trials of apocalyptic times. Through our individual experiences of tribulation we are pushed to root ourselves in something larger and more enduring than the conditions of our pain. We beat a trail through the thicket as we find our way to that "something" again and again. We cultivate practices that keep the way open, and learn to live from the insights and power we discover.

Wounds that Heal

In the Japanese art form *kintsugi*, broken pottery is repaired with gold lacquer. Rather than hiding the fracture lines, they are highlighted, affirming that the piece is more beautiful for having been broken. Restoration of wholeness is not a return to the pre-damaged state—that would be impossible—but the vessel is enhanced by honoring what it has been through. It's the same with us. What would it mean to honor our "broken places" with the tenderness and reverence of the kintsugi artist? To attend to each fracture and lovingly apply the golden balm of healing. To make visible, even celebrate, the map of our journey, allowing others to study it as an inspiration for their own. This is one of the most valuable gifts any of us may offer another, the sharing of our wounds and the learnings we have gleaned from them. Good eldering offers this—the golden traces of wisdom that have emerged through the healing of our wounds, and the ability to see the hidden wholeness in what society deems broken.

The wounded healer archetype, found in many cultures and traditions, is an expression of this. The wounded healer is not a savior, somehow over and above those who are in pain, but a co-traveler through the territory of suffering—offering accompaniment, insight, and care. Their own encounters with grief, loss, illness, or injury become their initiation as healer, and the ground of empathy and connection with those they serve. Indeed, their own wounding is the most important resource in developing their capacity to be a healing presence.

As a physician, Rachel Naomi Remen works with people facing terminal and catastrophic illness. Like me, she lives with (and has almost died from) Crohn's Disease. Remen writes,

Everyone alive has suffered. It is the wisdom gained from our wounds and from our own experiences of suffering that makes us able to heal. Becoming expert has turned out to be less important than remembering and trusting the wholeness in myself and everyone else. Expertise cures, but wounded people can best be healed by other wounded people. Only other wounded people can understand what is needed, for the healing of suffering is compassion, not expertise.[11]

Alice Walker observes that "[h]ealing begins where the wound was made."[12] This is not just a metaphorical and emotional truth, but a physiological one. In one of my past professional lives, I practiced medicine as a PA in pediatric oncology. I got to see first-hand how truly amazing bodies are, how they are designed for self-repair. In the body, the margins of a wound are the literal sites of healing—the place where Life is active. The cells on the raw edges of a wound are generative, multiplying to build new tissue and causing the wound to heal. The healing *grows out of the wound* itself!

It's easy to draw parallels to the collective healing process of social justice and transformation. From the sites of deepest societal wounding emerge the growing edges of change. Through the leadership of those most impacted by social ills new possibilities for collective wholeness take shape.

A ready example of this is the movement to defund the police and invest in community. This advocacy calls for non-police responses to non-violent incidents like mental health crises and traffic violations. It redirects a portion of the police budget toward programs that address the root causes of violence and crime, allocating those funds for health services, housing, jobs, youth programming, and the like. Studies have consistently shown that such an investment creates safer and healthier communities for everyone.[13] This call to "defund and reinvest" was elevated to national attention in the wake of the 2020 police murders of George Floyd, Breonna Taylor, and so many others, but the foundation for it had long been in place, led by organizers from the Black and Brown communities who have suffered the greatest harms.[14]

Martin Luther King Jr.'s 1967 sermon "Beyond Vietnam: A Time to Break the Silence," speaks to the possibilities that can emerge from the wounds of an unjust society. He said, "These are revolutionary times. All over the globe [people] are revolting against old systems of exploitation and oppression, and out of the wounds of a frail world, new systems of justice and equality are being born."[15] Recognizing and addressing the historical impacts of oppression, we can reach beyond them to create new systems that support the dignity and well-being of all.

Healing Together

Several years ago, I was in a counseling session with a client and the inner wisdom whispered: "The sites of your wounding are your greatest medicine for the world." And bless her, my client stopped me and asked me to repeat it, so she could write it down. As we considered it together, it rang true. It *is* our wounds, and the healing and transformational work that we choose to engage because of them, that shapes us into the instruments of healing for others. Note that I said, we *choose* to engage—because it *is* a choice. Wounding in and of itself does not automatically confer wisdom or healing capacities. It's how we engage our wounds, our suffering—how we engage oppression and injustice—that leads to the alchemy of new possibilities. Again, changing poison into medicine.

What are your places of deepest suffering or wounding, your places of transformation and healing? What medicine did that healing journey instill in you? What gifts, learnings, compassion, understanding, perspective, insights, capacities, strengths did you develop through your experience—even if the process is still ongoing? What have you gleaned that you can place in service to others, especially in the midst of the crises we face? Remember, our healing is never for ourselves alone.

The shape this takes will be different for everybody. Some may be called to the streets and some to bedsides. Some to be artists, poets, prophets. Some to work beneath the surface in the innermost dimensions of spirit. Some to craft policy. Some to educate and raise consciousness. Some to fight. Some to counsel and to heal.

What are you called to? What is your sacred wound medicine?

From the wound—from the wounded—comes the healing. People in recovery from addiction often make the best counselors for those trying to get sober. Survivors of domestic violence who have done their own healing understand in ways others never can what it takes to get free.

Through the seasons of my own life, and over years of working with others, I have learned that ultimately, nothing is wasted. Every experience holds the precious seeds of possibility and growth. It's useless to pass judgment based on the "snapshot" of any given moment because we never know how a story is going to end. It might be many years before the value and potential for healing becomes evident. And sometimes we may not get to see the beneficial impact on the life of another. But I have witnessed it enough times to have faith in the process.

Until we consciously recognize our need for healing, however, the healing process is hindered. Healing requires our active commitment, something denial inhibits. This is true on both the individual and societal level. Twelve-step programs for addiction recovery describe the dynamic of hitting "bottom" to break through denial. This provides the motivation for change. Bottom is the point at which the harmful impacts of a behavior or condition on self and others, the degree to which we are out of integrity, or the pain of things as they are, become untenable. The location of this threshold is different for everyone.

Denial is a protective strategy to keep us from seeing, from feeling, from acknowledging how dire things are—whether the "things" are substance use and addiction, unhealthy or abusive relationships, an untreated medical or mental health condition, or a social injustice. Telling ourselves that "it's not that bad" allows us to avoid the unknown costs of change. Yet at some point the balance tips, and the painful consequences of present conditions feel worse than risking the pain of the unknown. Not everybody reaches this point, and some become casualties of addiction, abuse, or treatable illness. And many, of course, become casualties of the larger societal denial of systemic injustice and ecological devastation.

Denying or minimizing our wounds keeps us isolated within them. Sexual abuse and assault, for example, is devastatingly common, but often held in secret. The trauma and stigma of being abused creates a chamber of silence in which we lock our pain, as we try to present a good face to the world. Shame, fear, disassociation, or threats from the perpetrator(s) reinforce our isolation, even many decades later. In my own life, and in the experience of so many of my counseling clients, I've seen how frequently we abandon the wounded parts of ourselves in order to function. The impacts of this internal fracture are far reaching. There can be a core feeling of unworthiness, of being damaged, dirty, or unlovable. Survivors may blame themselves, or suppress their memories and even question whether the abuse really occurred. The disassociation that began as a self-protective mechanism, a way to endure repeated trauma, becomes a way of moving through life.

The silencing of our wounds keeps us from finding strength in one another, from knowing we are not alone in whatever our experience of trauma may be, and from organizing for justice and collective healing. James Baldwin said, "You think your pain and your heartbreak are unprecedented in the history of the world, but then you read. It was books that taught me that the things that tormented me most were the very things that connected me with all the people who were alive, who had ever been alive."[16] Today it may be books, a podcast, or social media where we discover that connection.

The Alchemy of Lament

In denying the places of wounding we become complicit with a social amnesia that obscures patterns of domination, protects the agents of oppression, and hinders solidarity of and with those most impacted. Through the communal expression and shared witness of grief, public lament (even via a social media hashtag) can disrupt isolation and complacency, catalyzing a commitment to work for change. And lament can be a potent ritual of catharsis in both healing and social justice activism. In her book *Crisis Contemplation*, Dr. Barbara A. Holmes points out that lament challenges power structures as a collective response to tyranny and injustice. It gives us back our voices, allows the pain to escape, and offers a sense of belonging.[17]

We need to grieve the harms, losses, suffering, and pain that we and others have endured, to create supportive spaces to honor the wounds, listen to their stories, cry their tears, and release their fury. Only then can we integrate their wisdom. Only then is the energy that has been bound up in our places of accumulated trauma, the energy required to suppress the grief and numb our pain, or to stifle our rage, made fully available to living. Too often we want to skip steps in the healing process, to leapfrog over pain, grief, and lament, to focus instead on action. This is understandable, of course, but for both individuals and communities there is liberation in lament, healing in presence, and in being witnessed and held. This, too, is a crucial form of action.

Sobonfu Somé was a spiritual teacher from the Dagara people of Burkina Faso who regularly led healing retreats and grief rituals in the US. Among the Dagara, she explained, pain is not solely a personal matter. The whole community helps to bear the suffering, and the grieving person is surrounded with care and loving support. "Hanging on to old pain just makes it grow until it smothers our creativity, our joy, and our ability to connect with others. It may even kill us," she wrote. "Often my community uses grief rituals to heal wounds and open us to spirit's call, because there is a price in not expressing one's grief. Unexpressed hurt and pain injure our souls."[18] Communal grieving, she affirmed, offers validation, acknowledgment, and witness, and is thus healing and freeing for all.

As we allow ourselves to feel the pain of our individual and collective wounds, as we come together in communal lament, may our hearts be not only broken, but broken *open*. Broken open to new possibilities, broken open to reveal more courage, more creativity, more understanding, more love.

I think of our broken open hearts as the hard shell of a seed that splits apart within the soil to allow the emergence of roots, leaves, and the flowering expansion of Life. That, to me, is what the "open" vs. merely "broken" signifies: a heart that is vital and growing, rather than one that remains encased in its brittle protective shell. Rabbi Menachem Mendel of Kotzk, an 18th Century Hasidic rabbi wrote, "There is nothing more whole than a broken heart."[19]

The events of the world provide us constant opportunity to have our hearts broken open—in response to atrocity, yes, but also in awe of the beauty. The invitation (and the challenge) is to stay present to all of it, to allow our hearts to be as wide as the cosmos. If we look around, and all we see is suffering and evil and pain, we're not paying attention. But if all we see is sweetness and happiness, we're not paying attention. It's through the spiritual discipline of remaining awake to it *all*, of inhabiting the both-and rather than the either-or, that our hearts are most expansive and alive. This aliveness is what sustains us through the upheaval, reveals the medicine in our wounds, and nourishes our work for healing and justice.

---◎---

REFLECTION PRACTICE

I invite you to do some journaling on the questions offered in this chapter to see what insights surface:

- *What have been your places of deepest suffering or wounding, your places of transformation and healing?*
- *What medicine did that healing journey instill in you?*
- *What gifts, learnings, compassion, understanding, perspective, capacities, wisdom, strengths did you develop through your experience—even if the process is still ongoing?*
- *What have you gleaned that you can place in service to others, especially in the midst of the crises we face?*

We are cultivating within ourselves a transformative practice that helps us heal from what the world has been, while generating what the world will be. We must become accountable to our time, our earth, our species, our people, and our loved ones, from the inside out.

—adrienne maree brown

We cannot have a healed society, we cannot have change, we cannot have justice, if we do not reclaim and repair the human spirit.

—angel Kyodo williams

Spiritual self care is radical work when done with the intention to serve the liberation of all beings.

—Maryam Hasnaa

5

Soul Care

IN MYSTIC JUDAISM, IN THE TEACHINGS of the Lurianic Kabbalah, there's a story about the creation of the world. In the beginning there was only a vast sacred Darkness, the source of all life. Then the *Ein Sof* (the Infinite) emanated Itself into the world through ten aspects or qualities, known as the *sephirot*, by pouring these qualities out into vessels. But as the story is told, the brilliance was so great that the vessels shattered and their light scattered throughout creation. Our task as human beings is to gather the shards of light—the sparks of the Infinite wholeness—found in every being, every moment, every situation, and restore the Divine unity that is the foundation of existence. This is accomplished not only through the works of our hands—through service and activism—but also through the inner work of healing hearts and souls.

This process of restoration is known in Hebrew as *tikkun*, meaning to repair or make whole. You may have heard the term *tikkun olam*, the repair of the world. Alongside this is another component—*tikkun ha'nefesh*—the repair of the soul. It takes both, tikkun olam and tikkun ha'nefesh, the healing of the world and the healing of the soul; both are essential to wholeness. Estelle Frankel, a psychotherapist and teacher of Jewish mysticism, explains, "it is not possible to perfect one's own soul without also becoming deeply committed to the work of healing the planet, and since each individual person is a microcosm of the world, every act of tikkun ha'nefesh is of great, if not cosmic, importance."[1]

The "inner" work of personal transformation, and the "outer" work of social transformation and justice-making are not separate. Just as the in-breath and the out-breath together form a single respiration, one without the other is incomplete. Spiritual experience can both motivate and sustain activism. It fosters integrity, compassion, vision, and hope, deepening the place from which we work for collective liberation. And it replenishes us in the face of burnout, enlivening our connection with the sacred wholeness that animates all existence. In tandem with this, we can engage activism *as* a spiritual practice, transforming ourselves as we work to transform our world.

Healing as Movement Work

There is a long history of those who have served justice movements as healers and spiritual guides within an array of cultural traditions. Healing, whether physical, emotional, or relational, is fundamentally about restoring wholeness. And social justice is a matter of restoring wholeness to individuals and communities where systematic and state-sanctioned harm has been done. There is no real justice without healing.

Most of us come to social justice work with embodied trauma—personal, collective, ancestral. Indeed, it's often the pain of that trauma or the rage about its causes that brings us to participate in movements for justice. For effective and sustainable movements, however, we must be able to transform the wounds we carry lest we be destroyed by them. Both historically and in the present time of upheaval, trauma is weaponized as an instrument of domination. Healing, then, can be seen not only as a practice for our survival and well-being, but as a way to upend the workings of oppression and domination.

Recognizing the impacts of trauma and systemic violence on individual and community well-being, the architects of the contemporary healing justice framework lift up strategies for movements to address generational harm, exploring how we can heal even as we fight to end injustice. Grounded in a queer, abolitionist, economic, racial, and disability justice analysis, healing justice draws on traditional cultural practices to foster collective well-being and safety, and build power toward collective liberation. In their book, *Healing Justice Lineages*, editors Cara Page and Erica Woodland trace some of the roots of this work, centering Black and Indigenous peoples who have resisted centuries of genocidal oppression. The editors ask, "How do we draw from our ancestral memory, lineage, and ways of knowing to heal and be in right relationship to land, body, and spirit as integral to our political liberation?"[2] The answer is revealed in the stories, reflections, practices, and prayers they share.

A similar wisdom is found in the lived experience of people dedicated to creating liberative healing-centered futures. One of the most influential relationships in my own life has been my friendship with one of those people, historian and activist Dr. Vincent Harding. He and his spouse Rosemarie Freeney Harding were part of the Southern Freedom Movement, working closely with Martin Luther King Jr. and Coretta Scott King. They remained involved in movements for peace and nonviolent social change throughout their lifetimes. Both the Hardings were noted educators, scholars, counselors, and guides. Both were deeply in relationship with Spirit. In 1961 they founded Mennonite House in Atlanta as a hub for movement organizing and interracial hospitality. It became a place of physical and emotional healing for frontline activists.

Mrs. Fannie Lou Hamer was brought there to recover after the brutal beating she suffered at the hands of Mississippi jailers during her work for voting rights. Others also came seeking refuge, before returning to the demands of the movement.

In the early 1990s, by then living in Denver, the Hardings hosted Spirit & Struggle retreats, where African American activists from around the country could gather for healing, connection, and respite. In 1997 they founded what became the Veterans of Hope Project to document the lives and stories of spiritually committed activists from social change movements in the US and abroad, sharing those stories as a resource for younger generations.[3]

My own organization, OneLife Institute, was also committed to the holistic well-being of movement folks. For nearly two decades we hosted day-long Spirit, Sound & Silence contemplative healing retreats for activists and community workers in Oakland, CA. Along the way we developed our Sustaining the Soul of Activism program, and later added quarterly Healing Black Lives retreats to more specifically support the growing Movement for Black Lives. Through our work, we learned what the Hardings understood—that the power of compassionate connection is perhaps the most valuable medicine of all, and it is often the thing for which we are most starved.

Activist and educator, Shawn Ginwright describes the turn his organization made from a trauma-centered to a healing-centered focus. Ginwright points out that while providing an important lens, trauma-centered care emphasizes the impacts of harm, and can risk pathologizing the individual. He writes,

> A healing centered approach is holistic involving culture, spirituality, civic action and collective healing. A healing centered approach views trauma not simply as an individual isolated experience, but rather highlights the ways in which trauma and healing are experienced collectively. The term healing centered engagement expands how we think about responses to trauma and offers a more holistic approach to fostering well-being.[4]

As human beings we are shaped by the traumas we and our ancestors experience, but we are not defined by them. "If we carry intergenerational trauma (and we do), then we also carry intergenerational wisdom," notes author, activist, and former OneLife board member Kazu Haga.[5] Just as post-traumatic growth can follow the healing of our individual experiences of trauma, when we heal ancestral trauma—interrupting the inherited cycles of pain—ancestral wisdom becomes available to us in new and unencumbered ways. This wisdom then becomes the legacy passed on to future generations. Caring for ourselves, one another, and our communities is essential for creating powerful social movements that can be sustained over the long haul.

From Self-Care to Soul Care

In movement circles it's considered almost a given that activists will experience burnout. In many of my own networks, that badge of martyrdom was regarded as proof of one's commitment to The Cause, whatever that cause might be. "Self-care" (if it was discussed at all) was dismissed as self-indulgent and weak. How could anyone be concerned about self-restorative practices when there was so much injustice and suffering in the world?

Among some activists, spirituality is viewed with the same skepticism, as frivolous and self-centered. This mindset causes many people to become casualties of their activism, often forced to drop out of movement work—sometimes embittered, sometimes feeling guilty, almost always wounded. The more benign version—of *wanting* to take time for renewal but having it constantly preempted by the never-ending stream of crises—yields similar impacts. Physical and mental illness, exhaustion, addictions, and disruption of relationships are common "side effects" of activist life. The attrition this creates can lead to a kind of collective amnesia—a loss of the learnings and insight that come through decades of lived movement experience and multigenerational collaboration.

In recent years, more people—especially younger generation activists—are talking about self-care and seeing it as an integral part of movement work.[6] Those conversations, however, usually don't go deep enough. Too often I hear the term "self-care" used to refer to things that help us deal with stress or take the edge off our pain—a glass of wine or a beer (or a blunt) after a hard day, getting a manicure, or zoning out in front of the television with your favorite comfort food. At times these may provide needed relief, but it takes more than a spa day and a bowl of ice cream to sustain us in the midst of apocalypse.

Stress relieving and physically nurturing activities are vital, and can themselves be a matter of justice where such care has been systemically denied. But I hope we won't stop there. We need something more meaningful, more transformative, to stay connected to the place within that inspires us to do the work of our calling, and that allows us to bring our wisest, truest, most visionary selves to it on an ongoing basis. This is necessary for all of us, not just self-identified activists. We are, all of us, living in the struggle of these times.

Genuine sustainability is not simply about employing enough self-care practices to keep-on-keeping-on, continuing to work in the same dysfunctional and abusive ways. There is nothing transformational about that—for ourselves individually, for our strategies as activists and leaders, for our organizations, our movements, or the world.

So how do we move beyond the resuscitation model of self-care to root ourselves in something substantial and life-giving enough to support our flourishing? How do we sustain the *soul*—the spiritual center, the deeper vision, the inmost heart— that can inspire and guide our work, and every aspect of our lives, as we embody our commitments to personal and social transformation? We can reach beyond self-care to "soul care," engaging the practices that help us cultivate an inner connection to something greater than ourselves from which we can draw strength. That "something" may be one another, our ancestors or cultural heritage, Nature, a Higher Power, God—the Sacred, however each of us may understand it.

In OneLife's Sustaining the Soul of Activism curriculum, we began using the term *soul care* to highlight this distinction between activities that are primarily to relieve stress, and those that support a greater wholeness.[7] We described it as "the growth, development, and preservation of inner resources that allow you to meet whatever you are facing with _____ and _____." What goes in those blanks is unique to each person, and may even shift from time to time. For me, *love* and *wisdom* are the qualities I most hope and strive to embody. Taking those words, those qualities, we can set them as guiding intentions, making them our anchors, our touchstones. Indeed, they are already within us waiting to be given full expression.

With soul care we consider what practices and choices allow us to live from that place of connection to the Sacred, and meet whatever life brings with the best that is within us. What if we centered those practices collectively and integrated them into our activist movements? A communal spiritual practice of singing, prayer, and shared worship nourished the souls of those in the Southern Freedom Movement. And we see other collective spiritual practice today, for example, in the struggle for immigration justice, Indigenous sovereignty, and the Movement for Black Lives. By bringing spirituality into our activism, and embracing activism as a spiritual practice, we are transformed as we transform our world. The process is reciprocal.

The water protectors at Standing Rock Reservation working to stop the Dakota Access Pipeline demonstrated a powerful embodiment of this integration. Designed to carry crude oil across 1,172 miles, the underground pipeline violated sacred sites on treaty-protected lands of the Lakota and Dakota Nations, and threatened the water supply for millions of people living in surrounding areas.[8] When they were unable to obtain relief through legal means, water protectors established the first of several camps as a center for cultural preservation and spiritual resistance to the pipeline.

Within six months, many thousands of people had gathered, including members of more than 300 tribes from across the Americas, along with Indigenous peoples of other continents, and non-Native supporters. Prayer was the constant climate maintained in each of the camps, and prayer was woven throughout every action. After a particularly brutal assault on the water protectors by militarized police, the call went out for an international prayer vigil, to meet violent trauma with healing and love.

Indigenous musician, scholar, and community organizer Lyla June Johnston posted a video on social media announcing the vigil. She described prayer as "the force that allows us to bring in the ocean of resources from the spiritual world into this world, to help us achieve the impossible," and called on people to "create a global container around our brothers and sisters on the ground so that they may heal from the very traumatic experiences that they suffered."

She didn't stop there, but recognized the need to widen the circle of prayer to include everyone. She said, "Let us also pray for our brothers and sisters in uniform who inflicted pain on many of our water protectors, because they are of our human family as well, and they experienced the trauma of harming another human being yesterday, and they need prayer too."[9] The affirmation that even the perpetrators of harm are part of the sphere of compassionate concern is a powerful form of spiritual activism. It seeks to restore wholeness to those who may have forgotten their true belonging to the Sacred, and lost their ethical compass.

Another integrative approach can be found at the East Bay Meditation Center (EBMC) in Oakland. They offer meditation and spiritual teaching from Buddhist and other wisdom traditions, rooted in a commitment to social justice. EBMC centers people who are often on the margins of mindfulness communities—people of color, LGBTQIA2S+, and people with disabilities. Buddhist teacher and writer, Mushim Ikeda, is part of the core faculty at EBMC, and one of its founders. She developed an innovative year-long mindfulness training program for social justice activists, community workers, and transformative thought leaders. Participants in the program ground themselves in Ikeda's "Great Vow for Mindful

Activists," which reads: "Aware of suffering and injustice, I, _____, am working to create a more just, peaceful, and sustainable world. I promise, for the benefit of all, to practice self-care, mindfulness, healing, and joy. *I vow to not burn out.*"[10]

Spiritual 911

Burnout, commonly defined as a state of mental, physical, and emotional exhaustion, arises when the consistent stresses we experience and the demands upon us become overwhelming. Among activists, caregivers, and other frontline workers, trauma, grief, and hopelessness can also be contributing factors. There's a way that "burnout" is really too small a term for much of what we are experiencing today. To meet it requires more than just individual rest, but a lived relationship to the "something larger" that soul care and community connection can provide.

In some classes and workshops I teach on the subject, I suggest that people make a "Spiritual 911" emergency contact list. When I was growing up, there was one phone in the household, a rotary dial phone attached to the wall in the kitchen. Next to it, taped to the wall, was a list of phone numbers one might need in an emergency—the fire department, the pediatrician, poison control, and the like. The idea was that when your house was burning was not the time to have to start thumbing through the phone book for help.

Similarly, when we are traumatized, exhausted, or burned out, we may not be able to remember the things that open and restore our spirits. So it's helpful to create a written list you can refer to, and continue to add to, on an ongoing basis. You can even "crowd source" ideas by asking your friends to share the practices that they rely on to connect with the Sacred and replenish their souls.

It could be that you find connection through prayer or meditation, perhaps a particular song or piece of music that lets you breathe again, or maybe a movie that you know will make you cry and soften your heart when it has grown brittle. You might have a favorite tree that you visit, or a spot by the lake, or a particular poem or passage in scripture that opens the way to the Divine. Maybe for you it's gratitude, chanting, ritual, journaling or creative expression, or meeting with a wise friend who helps you tune back in to what is true. The key is to find what works for you, and to have enough soul care options that when one practice is not available or is not giving you what you need, you can turn to others.

The goal, of course, is not simply having a list of emergency practices to call us back when burnout takes its toll, but cultivating communion as a way of life—making the commitment to integrate these rituals of connection as part of our every day. Not using spirituality as an escape or anesthesia, but as a source of nourishment, insight, healing—of soul care. Taking time on a regular basis to enter the silence, to get off the treadmill of nonstop activity, and commune with the Divine is an act of resistance in a society that has made a god of materialism and in the process lost the real meaning of *soul*.

Communities of Care

Another common assumption about "self-care" I find problematic is actually a symptom of the extreme individualism and consumerism of capitalist culture. We live in relationship with one another and with the larger society. Our burnout and trauma occur within those constellations, yet when we are in need of restoration, we're treated as though it's our individual responsibility to go off somewhere and handle it. And because capitalism is extremely good at commodification, an entire self-care industry has emerged. Like so many things, this is both a blessing and a curse.

On the one hand, the self-care industry has elevated awareness about the need for care and normalized it as an appropriate part of our 21st century lives. On the other hand, it has been superficialized and given a price tag—one that is out of reach of many if not most people. This self-care industrial complex has turned activities of tending and nurture into products and services that are purchased, rather than organic components of relationship and community.

There is some dissent now in activist circles dismissing self-care in favor of community care. But they are not separate. A community (or a movement) cannot be healthy when its members are not; and no individual can truly be well when the collective is suffering. We are inseparably part of one another. I often tell people, no one can do your healing for you, but you don't have to do it alone. (As an introvert, I'm a great proponent of solitude and its importance, but we also need one another!) We heal through being present with each other: through sharing our insights and our pain, through witnessing and being seen, through compassionate connection. This, too, is a powerful form of soul care.

In Community with Nature

Community extends beyond our human family. We are part of the community of Life: of Nature and Spirit, of ancestors and coming generations. Just as we can receive care from other humans, we can receive it from Nature through the mutuality of relationship. We are surrounded by so much love, yet we are most often unaware of it.

I grew up amidst the concrete and asphalt of New York City, but even there were trees and grass and clover and dandelions in the park. And near one place my family lived, the Hudson River. Every autumn the leaves were painted with color, and a huge chestnut tree dropped its treasures for eager children to gather. The summer I turned ten we moved to a suburban town about an hour outside the city by commuter train. It seemed to me like the middle of the woods. I found refuge following a creek to a place hidden from sight. There I would sit for hours writing poetry and listening to the Earth, the Water, the Wind.

Today I walk in my urban neighborhood attentive to the warmth of the sun or the moisture of the fog, the movement of the air, the fragrance of flowers or herbs growing in street-side patches of soil, the cycling of seasons. I see the birds, the clouds, and the trees as part of cherished community. My relationship with Nature and especially with the Elements, and what I experience as the wise and loving intelligences within them, has become central to my spiritual life and to my healing work with others. Nature offers a potent medicine—especially needed in these times of layered daily and generational trauma, of intense despair, pervading injustice, and apocalyptic uncertainty.

The Elements are particularly good allies for helping to clear residual trauma and grief, and deepen our connection to the larger Life that nourishes all life. As you cultivate your relationship with the Elements, they will teach you their medicine. Remember that what we touch is the body of each Element, but there is a powerful ancestral spirit within each one as well. Meet them with respect, humility, and gratitude. In the Spiritual & Healing Practices section, near the end of this book, you'll find some ideas for ways you can engage the Elements to support your healing.

I have heard it said that in Nature exists the medicine for every ailment and illness—even the ones that haven't manifested yet. The cure is *already there* awaiting the need. This healing lies in both the specific chemical compounds found in plants and in the spiritual energies of Nature. It leads me to suspect that for the soul sickness of humanity, the medicine is already within us to treat it. We are part of Nature, after all.

The Practice of Awe

In recent years I've found myself organically drawn into a practice of cultivating awe as a form of soul care. Earth life is amazing, yet so often we don't bother to notice. Staying in touch with this amazingness helps me make it through the horrors that confront us daily. There is a physiological as well as spiritual basis for this. Feeling awe activates the vagus nerve, the longest and most complex of the cranial nerves, and the main component of the parasympathetic nervous system. It passes through our throat and voice box, and reaches into most of our internal organs, regulating our body's basic functions like heart rate, digestion, and immune response. Somatic therapist Resmaa Menakem calls it the "soul nerve" because it's linked to so many of the emotions that make us human— love, grief, hope, empathy, loneliness, compassion, and more.[11] Physiologically, through its effect on the vagus nerve, awe reduces stress, decreases depression and anxiety, lowers inflammation, and supports a healthy immune system.

Awe also fosters a feeling of belonging, of connection to something larger than ourselves—whether Nature, Spirit, or other beings (human and beyond)—the signature of soul care.

A professor of psychology specializing in the scientific study of emotions, Dacher Keltner's recent book, *Awe: The New Science of Everyday Wonder and How It Can Transform Your Life*, discusses what he and his colleagues learned through years of research. They collected 2,600 awe narratives from people in 26 countries, including all major religions (and non-religious folks), collectivist and individualist cultures, in democratic and authoritarian societies. For the study, they offered participants this definition of awe: "Being in the presence of something vast and mysterious that transcends your current understanding of the world."[12] They found that almost all experiences of awe fit into consistent categories, what Keltner has dubbed the "eight wonders of life."

The number one source of awe, researchers were surprised to discover, was moral beauty: "other people's courage, kindness, strength, or overcoming."[13] Witnessing these acts—things like people supporting one another through a devastating hurricane, or learning to walk again after an accident left them paralyzed—can move us to tears. Next on the list was what Keltner called "collective effervescence," a shared group experience like dancing in a crowd, being part of a political rally, or a ceremonial gathering like a wedding, funeral, or graduation. Through these experiences we feel connected with the people around us, and our nervous system synchronizes with theirs. Rounding out the list were the wonder and beauty of Nature, music, visual art, spirituality, the cycle of life (including experiences of birth and death), and epiphanies—those sudden flashes of understanding about the essential truths of life. Our bodies also respond to awe: sometimes with goosebumps, or getting choked up with emotion, or even with spontaneous utterances of "woah" or "mmmmmm" or "wow."

One of the simplest practices for accessing wonder, Keltner says, is taking an awe walk.[14] (Or it could be an awe sit!) You have likely already experienced this when a glimpse of natural beauty catches your eye. Elevating it to the level of intentional awareness can amplify the effect, allowing us to generate more awe in our daily lives. The key is bringing your full presence and childlike curiosity, beholding even familiar places and things with fresh perception. Imagine that you have never before encountered whatever-it-is. The vastness of sky or mountains can trigger awe, but so can the minute details of an insect wing or a dewdrop. We can do the same with other senses— hearing, smell, touch. (Each of us has particular senses that are dominant, our primary way of processing our environment.) If we allow our full heart-presence to meet the world around us, wonders are everywhere. In studies Keltner and his team conducted on awe walks, they found a measurable change in attitude, happiness, and well-being among people who took even one 15-minute walk each week for eight weeks.[15]

The benefits don't depend on big technicolor dramatic AWE, just small bits of awe tucked in the everyday moments of our lives if we are alert to them. Today, for example, I was moved by the surprise of new growth from a plant that I thought was dead, the slanting luminous quality of late afternoon light, a phone call from a friend right when we needed to connect, an aromatic whiff from the open door of a bakery that evoked a warm memory from my past. Yet awe is not only about natural beauty or positive experiences. Sometimes awe grows out of great hardship: witnessing another's courageous response to danger or suffering, companioning someone through the dying process, or observing the slow healing of a wound as tissues gradually knit together.

In practicing awe as a form of soul care, every breath, every bite of food or sip of water, every time we bathe, every touch, every conversation, every step upon the Earth, becomes an opportunity to embrace the sacred and to replenish our souls. Really, it's less about the activity itself and more about the consciousness and quality of presence we bring to it.

Are we seeing whatever-it-is as a mindless chore or a source of entertainment and escape, or are we entering it as a doorway into uniting our hearts with the Divine? If we can find what opens us to our inward center, we will find our center is connected to the Whole. Through this, there is a larger container to hold the pain or the rage, helping us to respond more skillfully to whatever lies before us.

Keltner notes, "Awe, by its very definition, requires openness. A nonjudgmental approach to mystery. And humility."[16] People who experience awe are more prone to compassion, to acts of generosity and care. Awe takes us out of our small selves and expands our sense of belonging to the magic of life; our boundaries dissolve. In this way, awe counteracts the fractured dualism that underlies so many of the world's greatest harms, and supports our work of tikkun—restoring the wholeness of the world and of our own souls.

_____ ◎ _____

REFLECTION PRACTICE

- *Consider the statement from OneLife's Sustaining the Soul of Activism curriculum, defining soul care as that which supports "the growth, development, and preservation of inner resources that allow you to meet whatever you are facing with _____ and _____." Fill in the blanks with the two qualities you want to hold as your sacred intentions.*

- *What are the practices that support you in embodying those qualities? What helps you connect with a deeper wholeness, that "something greater" from which you can draw strength? Begin brainstorming your Spiritual 911 list. Keep it somewhere you can turn to it easily and continue to add to it as you think of things. Ask friends to share their ideas. Include different spiritual practices, places in Nature, creative activities, readings, songs, rituals, and trusted people.*

One of my students wrote her practices and resources on slips of paper and kept them in a jar, pulling one out whenever she needed inspiration. Another student created a beautiful deck of divination cards, each with a soul care practice. There are no rules here. Incorporate a wide range of things, some familiar to you, some new. Some solo, some that involve other people. Some short and simple, some that require more time. Do something from your list every day. Continue to expand the ways you nourish your soul.

I have learned that the only way out of pain is to stop running from it; to meet it, sit with it, feel it, and see what it has to teach you.... The anger, the shame, the guilt, the rage, the frustration, and the fear are all outcroppings of the pain that we carry. The wound that is causing the pain that we are now feeling within our societies is not new. But how we respond to it can be. When properly addressed, this pain can mobilize us and lead us toward the transformation that we so desperately need. If we can find the courage to face it openly and honestly, it will heal us.

—Sherri Mitchell (Weh'na Ha'mu Kwasset)

Our trauma is not the entirety of our truth. It's not our resting place, or someplace we have to stay. It's not the definer of our existence.... Being intentional about my inner child work has shown me that I can reshape my narrative. I can create a new beginning for myself as I heal old wounds.

—Alex Elle

The past, the present, and the future, they inter-are.... That is why when you look deeply, and you know how to touch the present moment deeply, you touch eternity. You touch the past, and you touch the future ... and you can also transform the past, and transform the future.

—Thich Nhat Hanh

6
Healing Across Time

TO CONTRIBUTE THE FULL MEASURE of our gifts to the project of collective transformation, we need our wholeness. Unresolved emotions, historical trauma, and childhood abuse can pull us out of the present and leave parts of ourselves locked in the past. Our capacity for creativity, invention, healthy relationships, justice-making, and joy is diminished. The more we heal, the more completely we can live into our soul's purpose, and the more we can embrace the calling of this urgent season on planet Earth.

Time is not linear; it is fluid and multidimensional. We can access all of it from wherever we are within it. This awareness allows us to reach back to heal childhood and ancestral trauma, opening to the wisdom of the ancestors and our child-selves. It also allows us to reach forward, to be guided by our elder within and the yet-to-be-born generations—those who inhabit a future on the other side of the personal and collective struggles we face. If this all sounds too "out there" to you, remember we time-travel regularly! Whenever we ruminate about a past conversation, or worry about tomorrow or next year, we have left the present moment and located ourselves in a different time. It's another kind of portal.

As a counselor, I'm privileged to be invited behind the public image of many people, to walk with them through their difficulties. I consider it a sacred honor to be so entrusted. It's taught me how often the things we struggle with the most— and for which we may carry the most shame—are the same things that others struggle with. There is a universality to our pain. The particulars of our situations might be different (although there is a surprising degree of commonality here as well), but the feelings we experience are part of being human.

Each of us logs a spectrum of wounds, traumas, and hurts throughout our lives. Usually we find a way to tuck these hurts below the surface and carry on, perhaps hoping to leave the injured parts of ourselves behind. We might turn to self-medication to numb or distract with alcohol, food, work, sex, drugs, or social media. We may forget, disassociate, or minimize the importance of our hurts. In the short term, this strategy allows us to survive the trauma. However, in the long term, without healing and integration, parts of ourselves are missing. The good news is that healing is never out of reach. This is where the fluidity of time comes in.

Traveling Your Timeline

Imagine the trajectory of your life as a timeline extending from pre-birth through to your death and beyond. (Really, it's often more of a spiral than a straight line.) Every age of your experience is located on that timeline and can be visited—past, present, future. When we suffer a traumatic event, there's a way that a part of ourselves at the age we experienced that wound can become frozen in time, left in the past, so we can function in our daily lives. Multiply this by all the hurts we have experienced across our lifetime . . . all the abandoned parts of ourselves. To restore wholeness, to heal, we must reintegrate those parts. In my counseling work with clients, I talk about this as bringing those selves—our wounded children and younger adults of whatever age—home into our hearts in the present time. The harms they experienced may no longer be happening *now*, but until we bring all those precious ages of ourself into the present, they still inhabit the trauma. Where those younger selves live on the timeline, it is ongoing.

Conceptualizing time in this way, we can travel back to key ages when a hurt was experienced and work with that younger self the way we would with a beloved child or young adult in our "outer" life. To begin, first, just be present with patience, compassion, and attention. It may take a while before these younger selves are willing to talk. When they do, listen. Listen repeatedly. For as long as it takes. Remember, they may have been waiting 30, 40, 50 years or more for you to acknowledge and attend to them. You will have to earn their trust the same way you earn the trust of any traumatized child: through your consistent loving presence. Acknowledge their pain. Affirm them; *they survived*. Tell your inner young ones what you needed to hear when you were 3 or 8 or 12 or 25 years old. Trust your spirit to guide you. Be the parent they needed … you needed. When they (and you) are ready, invite them to come live with you in the safe home you have made for them in your heart.

These younger selves are not only reservoirs of trauma—they are sources of our spontaneity, creativity, imagination, vitality, and playfulness. Trauma stifles these natural gifts, and as we heal these creative, living sources become more available to us. The more of ourselves (our *selves*) we integrate, the more whole and alive we become.

This can be difficult and emotional work. I strongly recommend having a skilled therapist or spiritual counselor accompany you. I also encourage you to create a spiritual "container" for the process. For example, lighting a candle and saying a prayer at the beginning of your session, then extinguishing the candle and offering gratitude at the end, to bring closure to the experience before you reenter your day. Journaling is a valuable practice to process and capture any insights or learnings. If you feel the lingering residue of trauma, go outside and connect with Nature, or turn to one of the Elements practices at the end of this book. Music and movement can also help to clear and shift your energy. Check in and reassure your younger selves when you are experiencing something in the present that you sense might be triggering or retraumatizing to them. Invite them to share in your experiences of beauty or delight. Integrate them into your life. They are you.

The fluidity of time is not limited to the past; we can also travel to the future. Connecting with our elder selves can be a valuable source of guidance and strength. Being the adult for all our inner young ones can feel overwhelming when we're still in our own ongoing process of healing. We need someone we can turn to for support. While I absolutely encourage you to be in relationship with elders in your "outer" life, there are also wise ones within you. Envision the future self that has lived through whatever you are currently facing. How did they get through it? What did they learn in the process? What wisdom have they gleaned to offer you now?

I first encountered my inner wise one when I was in my 20s as part of a guided imagery meditation in a women's circle. To reach her required a long imagined walk down twisting paths through the woods. In the distance, I saw her on the other side of a bridge across a stream. Over the years she grew nearer. I could talk with her and seek her counsel. In this season of my life, I try to embody her as much as I can, although I often forget. And after forgetting for a while, I remember again. Growth is like that. Gradually we get closer to the self we are becoming.

Working with Our Ancestors

Through the fluidity of time we can reach beyond our own incarnational journey to the ancestors and coming generations. So much trauma is generational: patterns of harm that get passed down within families. The healing we do for ourselves, we also do for them. We are linked through both blood and spirit. When I work with clients on family patterns we send the healing back through their lineage, wherever it is needed, back to the first cause, and run it forward in time to infuse every generation. Like a long line of dominoes: tap on the first one standing in the chain and all of them go down, one after another. Or like switching on a sequence of lights, where each bulb ignites in turn until all of them are shining. Just as our healing benefits the others in our lineage, we can call on them to partner with us in the process. Perhaps because of adoption or estrangement, you don't know who any of your ancestors are. Be assured that they know you. You are connected, and whether or not you have names or photographs, you can reach out to them and develop the relationship.

Part of my own healing process was creating an ancestral altar as a place to honor and commune with those in my lineage who are no longer in the physical dimension. Different spiritual and cultural traditions have specific practices for how to go about this, and you may want to research the traditions in your heritage. I chose to keep it simple. A cloth defines the space, and on it I have photographs of my parents, grandparents, and great grandparents. I'm fortunate to have these, but you can substitute images or items that represent your people to you. You can include siblings, aunties, uncles, and other loved ones who have made their transition. Or start small and grow it over time. Come with humility, trusting Spirit and your ancestors to guide you. On my altar I also have the photographs of a few cherished mentors and friends who are no longer on the planet, a candle, a little bell, plus several small sculptures and items of personal and cultural significance.

The real medicine in it for me was bringing me into conscious daily relationship with these ancestors. The altar is on my dresser at the foot of my bed, so I greet them every morning and thank them every evening. Over the years, they have become a very present part of my daily life. In times of difficulty, I light the candle and sit down with them to talk things over and pray for help and guidance. The relationships are ever deepening and evolving.

Not everybody who has died is an ancestor, the same way not everybody older is an elder. These designations indicate a degree of spiritual maturity and wisdom. However, just as we continue to grow, so can those who have shed their physical form. A friend of mine who is steeped in ancestral traditions talks about one grandfather she had never met, who in Earth-life was a pretty unsavory character. He came to her in her dreams wanting to be added to her altar with her other ancestors, but she told him he wasn't ready, that he had work to do first. She also started to offer her own prayers and to do healing work on his spirit. After a time of this, his energy began to change and their relationship evolved. Healing the ancestors in our lineage is an important part of our own liberation, and it means the retained traumas and trespasses will not be passed to future generations.

In the first chapter of his book *Reconciliation,* Thich Nhat Hanh talked about the ancestors sending us into incarnation to heal the family line. He said maybe your parents didn't even want to have a child, but you were born because the ancestors sent you. Perhaps there are some things that can only be healed from inside their embodiment, and this is part of the reason for incarnation.

The Wisdom of Emotions

When old wounds get triggered, the emotions that arise can also pull us out of present time.[1] Emotions carry wisdom. They hold important keys for our wholeness, if we know how to listen and work with them. They force us to move beyond our analytical mind and into our heart. And we need this, for the planetary problems we face cannot be solved without the heart's understanding.

Some of us have been taught to think that certain feelings must be gotten rid of, especially uncomfortable or less pleasant ones. Yet often they are there to deliver a message or bring a gift. When we try to stifle them, they have to get louder to get our attention. The difficulties come when emotional energies are not able to fulfill their purpose and they get stuck or become overwhelming. We can dialogue with our feelings, and with the sacred intelligences behind them. We can thank them for their intent and cultivate a relationship that allows us to partner with them, bring attention where it is needed, and direct their purpose toward a greater good. In this way, our emotions become allies rather than afflictions.

As with the inner child and ancestor work, begin by centering in meditation and opening with a prayer or focused intention to consecrate the session and invite clarity. Ask the fear, rage, sadness, and so forth, what they need. Ask what their message is, their teaching, purpose, or gift. (You can write or record the answers you receive.) Rage may want to encourage us to stand in the authority of our being, saying "no more" to violation and injustice. Or it may be the defense against bottomless grief or overwhelming fear. Conversely, fear or sadness may be what masks our rage, seeking to protect us if anger is for some reason not safe to express. There is no rule of thumb. Which feelings we lead with and which are more buried depends on our particular emotional history and wiring. This is often a function of how emotions were dealt with or avoided in our childhood environment.

A counseling client I'll call Ani, came to her session and shared that she had been feeling almost overcome by anger. She was flooded by the pent up energy of all the anger that had been suppressed for so many years underneath her sadness. It felt to me like her anger had been locked in a dungeon—unavailable as life energy—and now it was loose. Ani found it a bit scary, but exhilarating. I reminded her it was the activated life energy, not the specific emotion of anger that felt like a high, and not to get attached to anger as the vehicle. Some people do, becoming addicted to the rush of anger, perhaps using it to feel empowered or avoid pain.

I encouraged Ani to work with the anger. To ask it what it needed, what message it had, what its gifts were. To honor it, love it, thank it. I suggested she make an altar for the anger so she could have discrete sessions with it, lighting a candle at the beginning and blowing it out at the end; establishing a boundary so the anger wouldn't leak into other areas of her life or into her relationships. This way she could be reminded it is a spiritual energy, and respect it as such. You may wish to do something similar with a sadness altar, a joy altar, or a courage altar, to honor the feelings and engage them in a sacred way.

Emotions, in and of themselves, are neither "positive" nor "negative"; they are a natural part of human experience. Their impact depends on how we relate to them and the wisdom with which we meet them. Do you have anger or does anger have you? Is anger an explosive uncontrollable energetic chaos that takes you over, wreaking harm and havoc, or is it an intentionally wielded instrument cutting away injustice to reveal truth and empower liberation? When we are in healthy relationship with an emotion, we can give it a holy assignment, directing its energy toward an intentional purpose. So ask yourself: do you have sadness, fear, or whatever the feeling … or does that feeling have you?

There's a linguistic element to this as well. In English we commonly say "I am sad," "I am lonely," or "I am anxious." In some languages, these qualities are described as something we feel or possess, rather than as something we *are*, defining our being. Thus, "I *feel* sad" or "I *have* fear." "I am" is such a potent declaration. I caution people to pay attention to what they say after that, and to ask if it's something they really want to claim as their identity. Your feelings of pain and rage and sorrow, and so forth, are real and must be honored, but they do not define you.

If a feeling is bigger than you can hold, ask to be held by something bigger—like Spirit, Nature, ancestors, cosmos, or community. Lie on the Earth and ask her to support and balance you. Ask Water to cleanse and renew you.

There's a Hindu teaching story, quoted by poet Mark Nepo, about creating more spaciousness within which to hold our experiences of suffering or pain—but it's true for any overwhelming feeling. In the story, an elder, weary of her disciple's complaints, directed the disciple to place a handful of salt in a glass of water, to stir it and drink. The student quickly spat out the mouthful! "Aaak! That's too salty and bitter!" they sputtered. The teacher then told the disciple to place the same amount of salt in a large lake nearby, to stir it, and taste the water. "It is fresh and sweet," the student said. The teacher then explained, "The pain of life is pure salt; no more, no less. The amount of pain remains the same, exactly the same. But the amount of bitterness we taste depends on the container we put the pain in. So when you are in pain ... enlarge your sense of things. ... Stop being a glass. Become a lake."[2] When we expand into our oneness with larger Life, the pain (or any difficult feeling) we experience becomes proportionally smaller and our capacity to engage it skillfully is increased.

Walking with Grief

I'd like to look more deeply at one feeling in particular: grief. There is so much grief in the world—both personal and collective—so much loss as we grapple with the mounting devastation around us. Grief has its own rhythm. It takes the time it takes and cannot be rushed. It's a natural process: a *process*, not an event. Every grieving will be different. Grief is not one single emotion, but an ever-shifting composite including pain, fear, guilt, anger, anxiety, resentment, longing, blame, loss, sadness, shame, self-doubt, separation, loneliness, remorse, judgment, isolation, confusion, despair, wistfulness, numbness, apathy, sweetness, gratitude, and even joy. It can be anything, and this is normal. The first and most important guidance I give to people who are grieving is to be gentle with yourself, and with others who may be sharing the grief— compassionate and patient, without judgment or expectations. I have seen so many people judge themselves for feeling sad "longer than they should," or feel guilty if they are not sad enough or for long enough, if they feel better "too soon."

In grief there are no rules and no "shoulds." There is simply no point to them. Grief doesn't care. Its waves will rise and fall, ebb and flow. Just like at the ocean, there will be "sneaker waves" that catch you unawares and sweep you into the depths. Ride the waves as best you are able. Breathe when you can. Ask for the support you need, when you need it. Remember also that griefs have a way of threading together with one another, and events in the present can trigger grief and trauma from the past. Sometimes it's the little griefs, the seemingly inconsequential ones, that unleash the torrent of stored and stifled grief. This is not a flaw; it's an invitation for healing.

Everything I described above, about working with emotions through sacred dialogue and creating an altar, pertains to grief as well. Ask grief to teach you how to walk with it. Listen to its wisdom and partner with it in fulfilling its purpose, rather than either resisting it or allowing it to completely take over. Receive your tears, when they come, as the sacred Water Element whose job is cleansing, purifying, and restoring. Call on the other Elements as needed to provide balance. Put your hand on your heart and send love to the hurting or frightened parts of yourself. What do they need in order to feel supported?

For some griefs, there will *always* be a tender spot marking the place of loss. I recall a book I read years ago, when I was doing a lot of death and dying work. The only thing I remember about it is the title, *The Absence of the Dead Is Their Way of Appearing*. Just that. The absence created by any loss—death or otherwise—is itself a presence. We most often think of grief as happening when someone dies, but we grieve many large and small losses all the time: the conclusion of a job or relationship, a dream or plan that ended in disappointment, children growing up, missing out on an important event, or changes in physical health, mental acuity, or appearance. In addition, consciously or not, we feel the pervasive collective grief of the world we inhabit—the extinction of species and the destruction of ecosystems, the ever more frequent mass shootings and police violence, human rights violations, war, genocide and displacement. And there are so many others.

We may feel things less directly when they happen "somewhere else," but in the context of oneness there is no somewhere else, no someone else. Our hearts are linked and we carry the weight of cumulative loss and suffering. The dominant culture teaches us to privatize our grief, to anesthetize ourselves through busyness, addictive substances or behaviors, consumerism, and entertainment media. Who and what does this serve? Whose agenda does it benefit? If we really felt the collective pain of humanity, of Earth and all our other than human kin, our hearts would break ... or break open. Broken-open hearts can be vital to restoring our humanity, increasing our aliveness, and catalyzing change.

It's never too late to heal. The "past" and "future" are available in every moment. Every moment is an opportunity to restore wholeness. This is powerful and important medicine for the collective heart-soul of us all. We can travel along our own timeline, and the timeline of human history, to process trauma and heal grief. And we can call on ancestors and coming generations as our allies in restoring a fractured world to wholeness.

◎

REFLECTION PRACTICE

There are a number of practices woven throughout this chapter. Several of them involve creating an altar as the spiritual container for healing work. Do you feel drawn to make an altar for a particular emotion? For your ancestors? For your inner young ones? Follow where you feel intuitively led, and build a simple altar as an act of love and reverence. (You can always add to it later).

Set aside some time when you can be uninterrupted to sit at your altar and enter into communion. This might be a meditation, a conversation, prayer, journaling, chanting, or song. I suggest you open and close your session with a clear intention, welcoming only that which comes as part of healing. Lighting a candle as you begin, and blowing it out to end your session is a symbolic way to create a boundary in time to hold your process.

If you need the support or guidance of a therapist, spiritual counselor, or trusted friend, please reach out to them. As I have said elsewhere, no one can do your healing for you, but you don't have to do it alone. We need one another, and that is also part of the healing.

A practical note: If your living situation doesn't allow you to build an altar that you can leave "out," you may want to create an altar kit. This is also great for travel. Gather your altar cloth (a scarf works well), a small candle (maybe one in a tin that you can close when not in use), and whatever photographs or other items represent the purpose of your altar. I also keep matches, incense, and a little chime in mine. Pack everything into a cloth bag or a small box—whatever you have. Then you can set it up for your session, and put it away afterwards.

PART THREE

Healing Separation

Applying a worldview of oneness to the process
of social transformation.

[W]e have to explore and interrogate everything that has caused us harm and created separation between ourselves and the land, ourselves and each other, and even inside ourselves—all of which is actually interconnected.

—Thenmozhi Soundararajan

When our fear overtakes our capacity for empathy, our capacity for love, we lose the ability to see the Human in the Other. And so the feared Other becomes for us a mirror of the Monster within ourselves, a hated being for whom no punishment is too great.

—Kai Cheng Thom

My message to the world is that we must come together and live as one. There is only one world; and yet we, as a people, have treated the world as if it were divided.

—Rosa Parks

———————◎———————

7
Mystic Oneness & the World of Dualism

IT'S A TRUISM THAT WORLDVIEWS create worlds. They inform how we relate to everything around us, influencing our social structures and systems, relationships, economies, governance, and values. The social and ecological crises we now face arise from a worldview of dualism, dividing all of life into contrasting binaries that are opposed to one another. In this belief system, people see themselves as separate from each other and from the natural world. This is the dominant perspective in modernity, but it is not the only perspective available to us.

The worldview of mystic oneness is rooted in reverent relationship, honoring the interdependence and sacredness of all life. Oneness is not some fluffy emotional feel-good that bypasses the demands of social justice and spiritual maturity. The imperative of oneness *is justice*, is healing, is wholeness. By understanding how division is constructed, we can deconstruct it. We can restore right relationship with Earth, other humans, and our beyond-human kin.

All Life Is One

The worldview of oneness, or at least a recognition of interdependence, has received more widespread acceptance in recent years. The internet, a global economy, climate crisis, and pandemics have offered physical evidence, while meditation and the popularity of various metaphysical and "spiritual not religious" beliefs have shifted the thinking of many. Cosmologists describe the common origin of every atomic particle in the universe as a stellar flaring forth some fourteen billion years ago. In the ever-recycling conservation of matter and energy, not only do the inhabitants of Earth literally share one another's breath, but our bodies and every manifest form are made from the same original stardust.

The theory of quantum non-locality (what Einstein referred to as "spooky actions at a distance") also points toward the unity and interconnection of all things. It observes that "once two quantum entities have interacted with each other, they retain a power to influence each other, no matter how widely they subsequently might separate."[1] This suggests that, since everything and everyone is formed from a common pool of subatomic particles, the minutest change anywhere has an effect everywhere.

Buddhist teachings of dependent co-arising and non-duality affirm a similar truth. Glimmers of oneness can be found in other religious traditions—in Hinduism, Sikhism, Baha'i, and in the mystic teachings of Judaism, Christianity, and Islam. A text of the Jewish mystical tradition reads, "The essence of divinity is found in every single thing—nothing but it exists.... It is present in everything, and everything comes into being from it. Nothing is devoid of its divinity. Everything is within it; it is within everything and outside of everything. There is nothing but it."[2]

Indigenous traditions from different cultures and continents have long understood that everything—humans, all of Nature, the cosmos, the ancestors and coming generations—is part of one sacred wholeness. Ghanaian mystic Brother Ishmael Tetteh explains that we emerge from Life as a unit of Life, the way a wave emerges from the ocean, rather than being created by something external to ourselves. The same is true for all existence; we are all expressions of one Source.

Yet, oneness is not sameness, and unity is not uniformity. In a universe that is characterized by such amazing variety, it's evident that whatever Intelligence is behind it all is not seeking homogeneity. We can look at it this way: the infinite diversity of existence emerges from an infinitely inclusive whole. Through our oneness with that common Source, everything and everyone, every expression of Life, is one with every other expression of Life.[3]

Things that may appear to be paradoxical or even contradictory to our logic-minds, in the mystic worldview are aspects of this inclusive wholeness. Polarities are complementary rather than oppositional. In Nature, day and night are not opposite forces, but complementary aspects in a continuum of dawn, sunrise, noon, dusk, twilight, midnight, and everything in between. The seasons—whether summer and winter, rainy season or dry—flow into one another in an endless progressive cycling. Even birth and death are not opposites, but both parts of the fullness of existence, taking place within the eternal ongoing spectrum of Life.

Constructing Division

Distinct from this harmonious complementarity, the dominant culture of the US, and much of the modern world, is rooted in a hyper-polarized oppositional dualism: absolute perspectives of us/them, innocent/guilty, winner/loser, male/female—and on ad infinitum. Oppositional dualism creates binaries out of spectrums, and opens a chasm of separation. There is little room for nuance or complexity, let alone the paradoxical both-and-ness that is so often the signature of the Spirit.

Division is intensified by a media-driven echo chamber of conspiracy theories and "alternative facts," intentionally stoking fear and enmity. The blatancy of the process—and its effectiveness—is instructive. By amplifying the construct of dualism, evil is projected onto a selected "them," while blameless virtue is held by an exclusive "us" and may be defended by any means. (Who qualifies as "us" and who is relegated to "them" changes with time and political expediency.) As part of this equation, the "other" is demonized and dehumanized—rendered disposable, without any ethical qualms. Throughout history wars, enslavement, and genocide have been energized by the depiction of human beings as animals, insects, or beasts. And what does one do with such creatures? Subjugate or exterminate them. The logic is chilling. But what is often missed here is that in dehumanizing others, the dehumanizer sacrifices their own humanity.

The reverse is seen in Indigenous cultures that respect all expressions of Life as relatives, treating each community in the natural world with dignity. In 2008 Ecuador became the first country to recognize and constitutionally guarantee the legal rights of Nature. "Rather than treating nature as property under the law, Rights for Nature articles [of the constitution] acknowledge that nature in all its life forms has the *right to exist, persist, maintain and regenerate its vital cycles.* And we—the people—have the legal authority to enforce these rights on behalf of ecosystems. The ecosystem itself can be named as the defendant" in a court of law.[4] In contrast, the US has conferred legal personhood, and all associated rights and protections, on corporations.[5]

Instead of understanding humans as part of the body of Nature, oppositional dualism sees Nature at best as an "environment" separate from us that we inhabit and, too often, as a supply closet of resources for extraction or a sewage system to receive our waste. This is not only lethal in its physical consequences, magnified now with the escalating climate disaster, but in the mental–emotional–spiritual impacts of separation from the natural world.

Fear and Othering

When we lose touch with our inherent belonging to Nature, to one another, and to generations before and yet to come, we are adrift. Domination works by severing these relationships. We are conditioned to feel separate from the wholeness of Life, and even separate from the consequences of our actions. Without relationship there is no sense of responsibility or obligation, no gratitude or empathy. Feelings of dislocation are both an effect of trauma and a cause of trauma. We can never *truly* be separate, even though that may be our subjective experience.

The formula for this constructed fracture is consistent. Stories are spun to generate resentment and fear of the other—whether that "other" is racial, religious or cultural, differently abled, differently gendered, or differently politicked. The scenarios may shift, but the themes remain consistent: a fear of *them* attacking or invading, fear of *them* taking what's ours, fear of a loss of power and position, fear of annihilation.

White nationalists, for example, see racial mixing, immigration, and the practice of genuine democracy (where everyone's participation is valued) as threats to their dominance and even their continued existence. Many believe white people are being systematically replaced by people of color. Dubbed "The Great Replacement Theory," the contemporary resurgence of this ideology draws on a 1973 novel by French author Jean Raspail. Depicting the destruction of white western society through mass immigration from the Global South, the book took hold among US white supremacist and anti-immigration groups in the 1980s and 90s, and inspired the 2011 book *The Great Replacement (Le Grand Replacement)*, by another French author, Renaud Camus.[6]

The theory has gained more mainstream traction in the US in recent years, promoted by influential pundits on right-wing media, and amplified by right-wing leaders of the Republican Party. It has been increasingly cited by white nationalist terrorists as the rationale for their acts of violence. During the August 2017 "Unite the Right" rally in Charlottesville, Virginia, white supremacists chanted "Jews will not replace us" and "You will not replace us" as they marched through the night carrying torches.[7]

Religious persecution (which is itself often racialized) can be found across time and within multiple faith traditions. For centuries Christian supremacists have sought to eradicate "infidels" or "heathens." The Crusades and the Inquisition, the physical and cultural genocide of Indigenous peoples throughout the world, vigilante violence and immigration bans against people perceived as Muslim are all examples of this. Men fear losing the dominance they are used to enjoying under patriarchy, and women have been "kept in their place" through brutality, sexual assault, and social structures that enforce poverty and subjugation. Economic othering has widened the gap between the wealthiest 1% and the majority of the world's population. These elite "haves" often feel no accountability to those at whose expense they made their fortunes.

The targets of polarization may change, but the dynamics remain the same. Modern capitalist societies have been manipulated into a hyper-individualistic culture of grievance, where any gains for the "other" are seen as threatening to those who hold relative power in the binary.

People are easier to control when they're traumatized, angry, and afraid than when they're at peace, hence the effectiveness of endless war, terrorism, and the use of media as a source of division. There's science behind this. In the brain, the amygdala is part of the limbic system. It's central to the perception of emotions like anger, fear, and sadness, as well as the control of aggression.

Another part of the brain, the middle prefrontal cortex, is responsible for problem solving, impulse control, moral reasoning, empathy, and the ability to foresee future consequences that result from current actions. Normally the prefrontal cortex helps regulate the limbic system, but when we are emotionally triggered the amygdala can release hormones that suppress the function of the prefrontal cortex. When this happens, our ability to reason and self-regulate is hindered. We lose our moral center, and can act in ways that are terrifying to others.

Trauma, PTSD, and chronic stress all increase the activity of the amygdala and decrease the activity of the prefrontal cortex.[8] The widespread prevalence of stress and trauma in society, combined with escalating fear for our physical, social, and economic safety set us up to be triggered. Add to this the strategic use of fear mongering and othering, and we can see the impacts in the world around us.

The implications of all this for collective social dynamics are striking. In his book *Jesus and the Disinherited*, Howard Thurman points out that fear "insulates the conscience against a sense of wrongdoing."[9] Acts of violence and domination are thus seen as necessary protection against the threat of the "other"—justifying huge military expenditures, mass incarceration, the caging of immigrant children at the border, ethnic cleansing, genocide, and the surveillance state. The way domination expresses, the form it takes, will simply morph until we uproot its foundation. True safety isn't found through stifling threat, but through fostering connection. The way to undermine the manipulative tactics of division is to restore our relationship with the whole.

The Power of Seduction

We've seen how fear and rage are manipulated to create social schisms, but empires also operate through seduction. Elites court the loyalty of their racial, gender, or religious constituents by offering a sense of superiority and pseudo-belonging. By fostering identification based on whiteness, for example, seduction intentionally disrupts the solidarity of poor and working people across the color line to overthrow an unjust economic system. White-identified working people may vote against their own interests—things like a living wage, accessible medical care, or clean air and water—seeking to preserve the social advantages of whiteness.

Seduction is an advertising campaign that glamorizes "lifestyles of the rich and famous," that determines worth (and offers it up for purchase) by the size of your TV screen, the model of your car, or the prestige of your job. Seduction operates as a prosperity gospel equating spiritual favor with material reward. By exploiting the core wounds that so many people carry—feelings of not ever being enough, of being unlovable or unsafe—seduction becomes a powerful weapon of control.

Unlimited corporate growth and executive profits are regarded as the measures of societal success, and technology is seen as the utopian solution to everything. This capitalist induced failure of imagination is not by accident. Capitalism manufactures and feeds off of people's feelings of chronic longing and discontent. Rather than human beings, we are re-branded as consumers, and sold a lie. And now we have been further reduced to "data," a commodity created by our digital footprints as we click our way through the internet. Our every trackable move is bought, sold, and traded.

As dualistic fragmentation thingifies life, we become insatiable in our greed and our emptiness—but you can never get enough of what you don't need. There is no amount of it that will satisfy the hunger, or assuage the emptiness. Because what we really yearn for lies deep within.

A Shift in Consciousness

The answer to oppositional dualism, like the answer to gridlock between political parties, is not finding a compromise somewhere in the middle. The entire system is faulty, based in a paradigm of fracture and domination. When the motivation of the system itself is to win more power and advantage for a narrowly defined few, rather than to provide for the flourishing and dignity of all, changing who holds power may temporarily impact who is in the most pain (and how much pain), but does little to shift the paradigm.

History teaches us that empires fall. They are inherently unstable, and their own excesses of extraction, division, and over-consumption eventually lead to their demise. Mahatma Gandhi is reported to have said, "When I despair, I remember that all through history the way of truth and love has always won. There have been tyrants and murderers, and for a time, they can seem invincible, but in the end, they always fail. Think of it—always."[10] Dr. Martin Luther King Jr. declared he had no doubt that Jim Crow segregation would die, the only question was how expensive segregationists would make the funeral.

For many years I took comfort in this. Yet I wonder now, given the vast historic scope of our dysfunction as a human species, and the millennia of our obscene cruelty toward one another and all creation, *does* "the way of truth and love" always win out? In the long arc of time, beyond our reckoning, perhaps. Certainly, that is my prayer. But it will depend on more than social restructuring; it will require a spiritual awakening and a return to right relationship, in oneness with Nature and all of life. Without this shift in consciousness, any progress we make toward a just and harmonious world cannot endure.

The Medicine of Mystic Oneness

Imprisoned journalist and activist Mumia Abu-Jamal asks,

> Where is the religion of Life? A religion that sets forth all the living as sacred? ... A religion that reveres all life as valuable in itself; that sees Earth as an extension of self, and if wounded, as an injury to self. We need a religion that recognizes the interdependence of [humankind] and this world; which sees that the atmosphere surrounding our globe is the same air

we breathe, and part and parcel of our lungs—that
Earth's water is no different from the saliva in our
mouths.[11]

Mystic consciousness, the consciousness of oneness, is the
awareness of belonging to something greater—not just as an
intellectual belief, but as a visceral relationship with the Divine
in its every expression. In this context the ruthless territorialism
of individual, corporate, or national empire-building is
unconscionable, and every act of oppression or cruelty, a
sacrilege. The mystic's primary allegiance is not bound to
country, religion, culture, or individualized selfhood, but to the
kin-dom of Life.[12]

The mystic ethos carries a rigorous ethical mandate: If all
life is one, then there is no "other," no "them" separate from
some constructed exclusive "us." There is no race or class or
nation, no river or blade of grass, that is not part of the Sacred
and ultimately, in the mystic's expanded vision, not part of
self. Within this paradigm any act of violence, oppression, or
exploitation is perpetrated against the whole. The motivation
to work for social justice and transformation, then, is based not
only on conscience or altruism, but on a compelling love and
reverence for the Divine.[13] (We'll look at this more in the next
chapter.)

A mystic worldview is rooted in this core belief: the
interdependence of all existence as one with an infinite Source
expressing within and beyond creation. Whether conceived as a
compassionate presence or an ineffable ultimate reality, it is the
unitive force within all that is.

The term "mystic" is so variably understood ... and
misunderstood. I usually begin my classes on the subject by
inviting people to name some of the common perceptions
about mysticism: definitions, stereotypes, associations that

come up when they hear the terms mysticism or mystic. The responses I receive are remarkably consistent, and often somewhat contradictory. Here's a sample. Mystics:

> Hold rigid structures and rules
> Have no structures or rules
> Act in the realm of magic and hocus-pocus
> Are given to spiritual rapture and ecstasy
> Are holy people with divine knowledge and wisdom
> Are isolated and introverted
> Have unmediated access to God

Mystics are typically considered to be removed from or unconcerned with the conditions of the world. They are regarded as rare or exceptional, with spiritual experiences different from ordinary human existence, or something belonging to other times and cultures. But is that really the case?

I invite students to read aloud from first-person accounts of mystic encounters by 20th century people living in the United States. Here are excerpts from two of them.

Jean Houston is a scholar and philosopher, best known for her work in the human potential movement. Here she has been describing her childhood aspiration to see the Virgin Mary, and her fervent prayer and attempts to evoke such a visitation—without success. One day when she was 6 years old, looking out her window at an airplane crossing the sky, she reports the following:

> Nothing changed in my outward perceptions. There were no visions, no sprays of golden light, certainly no appearances by the Virgin Mary. The world remained as it had been. Yet everything around me, including myself, moved into meaning. Everything became part

of a single Unity, a glorious symphonic resonance in which every part of the universe was part of and illuminated every other part, and I knew that in some way it all worked together and was very good.... I was in a universe of friendship and fellow feeling, a companionable universe filled with interwoven presence and the dance of life.[14]

Thomas Merton was a Trappist monk and writer. This experience at a busy intersection in Louisville, Kentucky, was recorded in his journal in March 1958. He recognized it as a turning point in his self-understanding and sense of mission, leading him to participate in anti-war and civil rights activism:

I was suddenly overwhelmed with the realization that I loved all those people, that they were mine and I theirs, that we could not be alien to one another even though we were total strangers. It was like waking from a dream of separateness.... Then it was as if I suddenly saw the secret beauty of their hearts.... If only they could all see themselves as they really *are*. If only we could see each other that way all the time. There would be no more war, no more hatred, no more cruelty, no more greed.... I suppose the big problem would be that we would fall down and worship each other.[15]

Pervading these accounts, and others that we read, is an atmosphere of awe and expansion, a feeling of wonder, love, and oneness with Creator and all creation (including all manner of people), and a witness to the "secret beauty" within everything and everyone.

In the academic study of mysticism, scholars parse out a taxonomy of different types, variables, and experiences. Generally,

I review these typologies with my students and then suggest they set it all aside. Rather than trying to dissect who is or is not "a mystic," or whether a particular occurrence qualifies as "mystical," I find it more helpful to talk about a *mystic worldview* or *mystic ethos* based on a belief in the oneness and sacredness of all that is. Accepting this worldview does not require someone to have had a personal transcendent encounter. Indeed, there is a wide spectrum of mystic experience: from self-dissolution with a complete loss of awareness of time and surroundings, to simply smelling a flower and having an expanded heart-opening connection—with the flower, with Life, with Spirit. Communion with the Divine in the world of Nature is a common experience that many people have had, often in childhood, and not regarded as "mystical."

We have been so conditioned by a hierarchical society that we are quick to privilege the more dramatic mystic encounters as real or valid, and dismiss the many smaller glimpses of oneness. Think of it like this: the ocean water in the waves of a tsunami may carry more power than one of the millions of smaller waves that daily lap the shore, but they are not more "ocean-y." They are all comprised of the same stuff.

The mystic worldview recontextualizes our sense of belonging: we recognize the universe as home and all its expressions our kin. The unity of each individual with all-that-is makes everything part of "self" in a profound and literal way. This consciousness of oneness has the potential to shift not only how we conceive of our location in the cosmos, but how we behave toward all life. Such a relationship can engender a feeling of empowerment, and of responsibility to the whole.

Tapping into the mystic frequency, we connect with a huge energy of alliance. Our elders the trees, the mountains, the birds, the mycelium, the whales, the Earth herself, all operate from the remembrance of oneness. This is the majority consciousness on the planet! As far as I can tell, only we humans have lost our way, yet not even all of us. When I see it like this, it no longer feels like quite such an impossible task to turn the tide: We are in league with all of Life.

REFLECTION PRACTICE

- *How do you see the ideology of oppositional dualism operating in current national and international events? Who does this benefit? Who does it harm?*
- *How does this ideology operate in your own life and attitudes?*
- *Have you ever had experiences of awe or oneness on the spectrum of mystic encounter as I've described it here? Are there ways that experience changed you, or revealed something that you continue to carry with you?*
- *Take some time to journal about one of those experiences, write a poem or haiku, create some art or music—whatever feels right to you as a way to honor your encounter.*

If we care about the spirit, we cannot avoid concern with the here and now. The spiritual is about the social, the mystical is also about the political. The cosmic in us has to be about both changing the human and changing the world of which we are a part. The healing inside and the healing of the world are wrapped up in one another.

—Omid Safi

Mysticism, if it is anything, reveres and works to sustain the sacredness of the world.... Genocide, racism, and sexism, as examples, reflect a direct violence against and rejection of God's living presence in the diversity of creation. Crimes against humanity are also crimes against divinity; similarly, whatever protects life contributes to the spiritual flourishing and happiness of all sentient beings.

—Beverly Lanzetta

To realize that we are not simply physical beings on a material planet, but that we are whole beings, each a miniature cosmos, each related to all of life in intimate, profound ways, should radically transform how we perceive ourselves, our environments, our social problems. Nothing can ever be isolated from wholeness.

—Vimala Thakar

8

Mystic Activism

AT THE AGE OF SIX, VIMALA THAKAR ran away from home in search of God. As a young child she was constantly asking, "Where is God? How can I find God?" Someone told her God was in the forest, so off she went. She and a friend tied some snacks in a kerchief and walked all day, many miles for young legs, calling "Where are you God? Come out; we have come to meet you."[1] As evening drew near, they saw her friend's father driving toward them. Her friend gladly got into the car, but young Vimala resisted, steadfast in her quest. The scar on the man's hand where she bit him was an enduring testimony to her tenacity.

Consumed by a burning hunger for the Divine throughout her life, she devoted herself to spiritual inquiry and liberation. As a young woman Thakar became a leader in Vinoba Bhave's Land Gift Movement, traveling on foot across India, from village to village, convincing wealthy land owners to voluntarily share part of their land with the poorest landless farmers. Through this effort, millions of acres changed hands in what was known as the Bloodless Revolution. Then in 1956 she began a series of pivotal meetings with philosopher Jiddu Krishnamurti. With his encouragement, she traveled the world as a spiritual teacher for the next thirty years, before spending the last twenty years of her life teaching from her home in India. During that time she was also involved in development projects with local villages to foster self-sufficiency and environmental sustainability.

Thakar's life exemplified the twin commitments of inner and outer transformation. She maintained that only by addressing both—the spiritual and the social—can we bring about meaningful wholistic change. Her activism was infused with the spiritual assertion that all Life is one. She wrote, "Life is not fragmented; it is not divided. It cannot be divided into spiritual and material, individual and collective. We cannot create compartments in life—political, economic, social, environmental. Whatever we do or don't do affects and touches the wholeness. . . . We are wholeness, and we move in wholeness. The awareness of oneness refuses to recognize separateness. . . ."[2]

Across history there have been those in whose lives the mystic and the prophetic come together: People from every faith and culture whose vision of the essential oneness and sacredness of all-that-is leads them to work to alleviate suffering and oppression as agents of social change. During my doctoral research in the late 1990s and early 2000s, I began describing them in my notes as "mystic-activists."[3]

Although an activist response to the mystic encounter is by no means universal, it's not uncommon to find mention of certain individuals—most often Mohandas Gandhi, Martin Luther King Jr., and Mother Teresa—as "socially engaged mystics." Extending the list beyond this trinity, people often think of Dorothy Day and Thomas Merton, or perhaps the Dalai Lama. The consistency of those named confirms the existence of an identifiable type. They are usually viewed as rare and exceptional—hallowed beings beyond what can be expected of regular folk—but the synergy between a spirituality rooted in oneness and engagement in social issues is quite organic. As dualism and separation are transcended, we feel the pain of injustice wherever it is found, and we are compelled to respond.

In the previous chapter, we looked at how the term "mystic" can be so variably understood as to be problematic. I talked instead about a mystic worldview, ethos, or consciousness. Similarly, I'm less concerned here with categorizing individuals as "mystic-activists" than describing a lived commitment to justice, healing, and social transformation that grows out of a consciousness of oneness. In the mystic worldview, nothing is outside the realm of the Sacred. Even if humans act in ways that desecrate—failing to respect the inherent dignity and worth of one another or of the Earth—that doesn't alter the fundamental nature of existence, or our responsibility to honor the sacredness within everything and everyone through our actions.

In my classes on mysticism and social change we study a wide variety of "for instances" to see what the intersection of activism and a spirituality of oneness might look like in the lives of others. But even more important is for students, and each of us, to discover what it looks and feels like in our own lives—in the particulars of our commitments, faith, and social location.

Mysticism & Social Change

The inner work of spiritual awakening is mutually synergistic with social action. Too often these have been framed as competing priorities. One side sees spirituality as self-indulgent in the face of global injustice and calamity, arguing that precedence must go to activist struggles. The other side says that spiritual transformation must come first, and with inner liberation the issues of the world will be resolved. However, our problems cannot be solved by just one or the other alone: both are essential. Mystic activism recognizes the socially transformative impacts of inner awakening, and the spiritual necessity to work for a better world.

Again, unless *we* are changed—our individual and collective consciousness is changed—we will continue to reproduce the same dynamics of dysfunction and domination in the collective life of our social structures. A social revolution alone is not enough, a spiritual revolution is also needed.

Throughout his professional life, Howard Thurman offered a clear and consistent articulation of what I am calling mystic activism. His words resonated with me deeply, and affirmed the path of my own intuitive calling. Thurman said,

> The mystic's concern with the imperative of social action is not merely to improve the condition of society. It is not merely to feed the hungry, not merely

to relieve human suffering and human misery. If this were all, in and of itself, it would be important surely. But this is not all. The basic consideration has to do with the removal of all that prevents God from coming to [fullness] in the life of the individual. Whatever there is that blocks this, calls for action.[4]

Here, Thurman is not talking about charity or altruism, but *liberation*.

You may remember from my discussion of illness and suffering, that Thurman defines spiritual disciplines as those practices through which we remove the barriers to our "inner altar," our place of communion with the Divine. I mentioned some of the things we might commonly think of—prayer, meditation, the study of sacred texts—and explained why he considered suffering as a discipline of the spirit. Thurman extends the list further, to include *social activism as a spiritual discipline*! He recognized that conditions of social and economic injustice can block both the oppressed *and the oppressor* from, as he put it, "free and easy access" to that altar. He acknowledged, "It is much easier, within the context of mystical piety to identify with the sufferer, the hungry, the poor, the neglected, than with those whose power, privilege and insensitivity are largely responsible for the social ills. But I must not forget that the ill a man does to others stands between that man and his own inner altar."[5]

Oppression and injustice harms everybody, hindering both the persecuted and the perpetrator from coming into full relationship with the wholeness of Life, and expressing their authentic gifts and purpose. The significance of this from a social justice standpoint is clear: If the oppressor is not transformed, neither can society be transformed in a lasting way. From the perspective of spiritual oneness, our liberation is bound up together.

The South African *ubuntu* theology of Archbishop Desmond Tutu offers a clear example of this principle in action. Regarding whites upholding racial apartheid, he affirmed "they too are God's children, even though they may be our oppressors, though they may be our enemies. Paradoxically, and more truly, they are really our sisters and our brothers, ... and their humanity is caught up in our humanity, as ours is caught up in theirs."[6] Tutu notes, "When we see others as the enemy, we risk becoming what we hate. When we oppress others, we end up oppressing ourselves."[7]

In the Nguni languages of southern Africa, ubuntu literally means "human-ness," referring to human goodness or human kindness. It affirms our interdependence as human beings, demanding that we be our best selves with one another. Tutu explained that in ubuntu people know "they belong to a greater whole, and know that they are diminished when another is humiliated, is diminished, is tortured, is oppressed, is treated as if they were less than who they are."[8] Because all people are expressions of the Divine, "injustice, racism, exploitation, and oppression are to be opposed not as a political task, but as ... a spiritual imperative."[9]

A similar perspective was clear in the framing of the US Southern Freedom Movement, a movement that Dr. Thurman was instrumental in nurturing. Although it has more often been called the Civil Rights Movement, I have heard movement elders (many now ancestors) bristle at that term. To them it was a spiritual liberation movement, through which civil rights would be addressed.

The mission statement of the Southern Christian Leadership Conference, an organization originally led by Dr. King, was "to redeem the soul of America" with the ultimate goal of creating beloved community.[10] King wrote, "Only through an inner spiritual transformation do we gain the strength to fight vigorously the evils of the world in a humble and loving spirit."[11] In his sermon, "Beyond Vietnam," delivered exactly one year before he was assassinated, King called for "a radical revolution of values" to counter "the giant triplets of racism, extreme materialism, and militarism" plaguing the nation.[12] This interweaving of inner and outer, spiritual and social, is central to mystic activism.

Henri Nouwen, a Dutch author and priest, believed that those "who walk the mystical way are called to unmask the illusory qualities of human society."[13] He considered mysticism and revolution to be two aspects of the same attempt to bring about radical change. Radical means going to the root or the primary source. We need radical approaches to white supremacy. Radical approaches to capitalist exploitation and warmongering. Radical approaches to environmental devastation. The root of these societal ills is found in consciousness.

Transforming Consciousness

By "consciousness" I mean our fundamental beliefs about who we are, why we are here, and the nature of Life. Consciousness is not an abstract thing. It defines the narrative that shapes everything else in our experience, the story through which we construct meaning—individually and collectively. Out of that narrative, that consciousness, we create and engage the world. This is part of the power of art and music and poetry, of imagination and dreaming. They help us conceive new narratives, and new worlds rooted in ancient and visionary Truths.

Mysticism moves us out of oppositional dualism and into a consciousness of oneness. This paradigmatic shift is essential for us to return to living in reverent balance with all of Life. The disaster-ridden world we now inhabit is a product of dualism and fragmentation. That consciousness, no matter how clever, cannot change our current trajectory. As the oft-repeated observation from Einstein cautions: *no problem can be solved with the same consciousness that created it.* The ethos of mystic oneness opens fresh perspectives and approaches for wholistic transformation.

A cosmology of oneness suggests that as I transform *my* consciousness, it has an influence on everything and everyone. And as each individual consciousness transforms, there arises a wave of transformation in the collective consciousness that can tip the balance toward a new reality. The Sarvodaya Shramadana Movement in Sri Lanka, led by A. T. Ariyaratne, employed this principle in their efforts to end the country's longstanding civil war. In the late 1990s and early 2000s they held large scale events gathering hundreds of thousands of people from several faith traditions to sit together in meditation for peace. Their goal was to shift the collective consciousness of that country— what Dr. Ariyaratne called the "psychosphere."

The name *Sarvodaya Shramadana* comes from the Sanskrit, *sarva* meaning "all" or "embracing everything," *udaya* meaning "awakening," and *shramadana* a "gift of labor." Combining Buddhist precepts with the teachings of Gandhi, the Sarvodaya Movement has implemented programs in Sri Lanka and internationally in education, health care, agriculture, renewable technology, community development, and peacemaking— employing a spiritually-based self-help method in their work for social change.[14]

A mystic approach to social action invites us to call on energies beyond our finite selves to transmute the injustices of the world. Howard Thurman described this in a 1953 sermon entitled "Those Who Walked with God." In it, his delivery is passionate, and somewhat defensive. As the renowned Thurman scholar Dr. Luther Smith shared with me, although Thurman is talking about "the mystic" here, he is really talking about *himself*, and responding to the criticisms he received for focusing on spirituality when some thought he should be more involved in leading Movement work.[15] Addressing the mystic's role in social justice struggles, Thurman explained,

They felt that the way to do it is to move underneath the foundation that stabilizes the evil order. And if you move at that level, when you stir, everything that is above you will begin to crumble and fall; because there is no power *less* than the power of God that is capable of withstanding the power of God. Therefore, if I can release as a living channel, the living energy of *God* into the situation, anything that is less than that that is in the situation will be destroyed.

That is what the mystic does with social action. He is no coward, sticking his head in the sand, praying to God because he's scared or because he doesn't have the nerve to do anything else. But he is sure that he is in touch with terrible energy, *terrible energy*. And if his life can be a point of focus through which that energy hits its mark in the world, then the redemptive process can work. And that is why the way of the mystic is so difficult, and yet in some ways so simple.[16]

When I learned specific practices from Brother Tetteh to heal the collective soul, what he calls the soul of humanity, I felt that I had found a tool to do the energetically transformative work that Dr. Thurman was describing. The practices focus not only on clearing trauma where collective harm and abuse have been experienced—genocide, war, slavery, racial and sexual violence, and so on—but also healing the soul-sickness of the perpetrators, thereby shifting the foundations of harm.

As a life-long social justice activist, this union of mystic spirituality with social transformation resonates with me profoundly. As a white-bodied person in the United States—the belly of the beast of global domination and racialized oppression—I feel it as a responsibility. Over time I have come to understand that there is a level of access we have from our embodied location as humans—and part of the soul of humanity—to influence human consciousness. And since humans are the architects of fracture and division, we are uniquely positioned to shift it from the inside.

The Activism of Interbeing

There are many more examples of how a spirituality rooted in oneness informs the work of justice-making. During the war in Vietnam, Zen Master Thich Nhat Hanh and his order of monks and nuns were persecuted for refusing to take sides. They ministered to the suffering of communist and anti-communist forces alike, and for this Nhat Hanh was exiled from his homeland for 40 years. He coined the term "engaged Buddhism" and founded the Order of Interbeing, based on the principle of *advaya* (non-duality) and the bodhisattva precepts. He taught mindfulness as a way of living in which we see our oneness—our interbeing—with all that is, and that this insight moves us to ethical action. With interbeing there is an understanding that everything is part of everything else in the universal order. Nhat Hanh explained, "we belong to each other; we cannot cut reality into pieces. The well-being of 'this' is the well-being of 'that,' so we have to do things together. Every side is 'our side'; there is no evil side."[17]

The discipline of mindfulness calls us to look searchingly to discover where we may be contributing to the very conditions we deplore—violence, poverty, injustice, environmental destruction. Seeing the significance of our every choice and action on the web of life brings a sense of responsibility, but also provides the agency for change.

A bodhisattva is one who, having come into their own enlightenment, vows to carry on in service to the world until all beings are free from suffering and oppression. Traditionally this refers to the celestial beings of the Buddhist pantheon like Quan Yin, the bodhisattva of compassion, but the archetype has been adopted by socially engaged Buddhists as inspiration for their own commitment to sacred activism. The bodhisattva vow is taken by a practitioner ready to dedicate themselves to the benefit of others, the liberation of all sentient beings.

Shantideva, an eighth-century Buddhist monk, philosopher, and poet, wrote *A Guide to the Bodhisattva's Way of Life*. It includes a prayer that portrays the bodhisattva commitment, and is said to be among the Dalai Lama's daily devotions. Here's a particularly poetic rendering:

> May I become at all times, both now and forever
> A protector of those without protection
> A guide for those who have lost their way
> A ship for those with oceans to cross
> A bridge for those with rivers to cross
> A sanctuary for those in danger
> A lamp for those without light
> A place of refuge for those who lack shelter
> And a servant to all in need
> For as long as space endures,
> And for as long as living beings remain,
> Until then may I, too, abide
> To dispel the misery of the world.[18]

What does it mean to live into a vow like this in the midst of the monumental suffering of a collapsing world?

We have to remain present—with ourselves, with one another, and with the Divine. This includes being present to both the current and historical magnitude of trauma and injustice, *and* to a vision of the healing and beauty that is possible. To hold the simultaneous both-and-ness of it all. Our capacity as agents of transformation is amplified through our belonging within the web of all being. Just as with a spider's web, where a tap anywhere transmits vibration to the whole of it, every touch upon the web of Life vibrates everywhere. Mystic activism is rooted in this all-pervading interconnection.

Vimala Thakar points out, "the inner life is not a private or personal thing; it's very much a social issue. The mind is a result of collective human effort. There is not your mind and my mind; it's a human mind. It's a collective human mind. . . ."[19] She affirms that "we share creativity, intelligence, and unlimited potential with the rest of the cosmos" and that this can (and must) be engaged to bring about inner and outer transformation.[20] Thakar writes, "Revolution, total revolution, implies experimenting with the impossible. And when an individual takes a step in the direction of the new, the impossible, the whole human race travels through that individual."[21] Love, she says, "is the force of total revolution."[22]

The mystic ethos inspires an ethic and an activism driven by love, and prompts a prophetic engagement with the world. It calls us to become conscious of the entirety of our thought, belief, and action: to seek the places of inconsistency and consider them in light of the larger questions about the meaning of life and the core of our values. Love is the antidote to the construction of otherness.

Rooted in Love

"The moment we choose to love we begin to move against domination, against oppression," wrote scholar and activist bell hooks. "The moment we choose to love we begin to move towards freedom, to act in ways that liberate ourselves and others."[23] Hooks references the love ethic undergirding the activism of Dr. King and the Southern Freedom Movement, and points out that the power of the movement was its emphasis on freedom and justice for *everyone*. It was not bound by dualistic "us and them" thinking, but affirmed an expansive inclusivity.

In Thurman's classic text, *Jesus and the Disinherited* (a book foundational for King and others in the Movement), he posits Love as the remedy for what he called the three hounds of hell that underlie the dynamics of oppression—fear, deception, and hate. Love is employed as a kind of spiritual aikido (my term, not his) to undermine the social hierarchy of oppression and enable authentic relationships between equal souls.

Justice work, as I have noted, *is* the work of healing. And as we engage it from the mystic ethos of oneness, it must be rooted in love. This is a volitional love. Love not as reactive emotion or fondness, but as disciplined soul force. Its cultivation changes our hearts. It makes us more compassionate, more patient and receptive with one another—and hopefully also with ourselves. It makes us more open to all the expressions of Life, and more protective of them.

Gloria Anzaldúa must have been feeling something like this when she wrote,

> With awe and wonder you look around, recognizing the preciousness of the earth, the sanctity of every human being on the planet, the ultimate unity and interdependence of all beings—*somos todos un país.* Love swells in your chest and shoots out of your heart chakra, linking you to everyone/everything. . . . You share a category of identity wider than any social position or racial label. This *conocimiento* motivates you to work actively to see that no harm comes to people, animals, ocean—to take up spiritual activism and the work of healing.[24]

This is the foundation of mystic activism: a recognition of the Divine as the unifying essence within all, and a compelling love for the multiplicity of Life's expression that inspires our commitment to work toward justice and wholeness.

―――――― ◎ ――――――

REFLECTION PRACTICE

As we explore the intersection of mystic experience (or the worldview of oneness) and the work of social action, what might this look like in the context your own life and commitments? How might you embody the synergy between personal transformation and social transformation, between contemplation and action?

- *Take some time to journal about how a worldview of oneness would shift the way you engage in activism or community service, or even your social media posts. What would change if you stopped perpetuating the "us" versus "them" binary? How would it affect your choices, actions, methods, attitudes, motivations, etc.?*
- *Experiment with embodiment. Begin a consistent contemplative practice that invites you into heart-opening union with the larger Life that breathes through everything. (Look back at the Soul Care chapter if you need some inspiration, or check out some of the meditations in the Practices section at the end of this book.)*
- *If you are already involved in activism or community service, challenge yourself to intentionally bring this expansive consciousness into your social action. If you are not already engaged, find a way to get involved, and practice the integration of spirit and action.*
- *Please note that this is not a one-time thing. It takes ongoing practice to cultivate these "spiritual muscles" and develop the habit of awareness, but the more you practice this intention, the more it will become an organic part of how you move in the world.*

The revolutionary sees his task as liberation not only of the oppressed, but also of the oppressor.

—Steve Biko

In the current historical moment, with multiple crises coming to a head, white people have a pressing need to connect with our basic humanity and separate ourselves from the status-quo-supporting roles we are socialized and manipulated to play.... We need to know ourselves as children of this earth and members of a human family who, like everyone else, have an undeniable stake in building a just and life sustaining society in which we all can thrive.

—Eleanor Hancock

Building a culture of belonging, care and love is at the very center of dismantling white supremacy culture.

—Jardana Peacock

———————— ◎ ————————

9
Healing Whiteness

A MYSTIC APPROACH TO SOCIAL TRANSFORMATION compels us to focus not only on the oppressed, but on those who perpetrate and perpetuate oppression. In a cosmology of oneness, our humanity—and even our survival—is bound up together. As we seek to address the fractures that plague our world, our path to healing must include an honest, rigorous, and heart-centered reckoning with white supremacy. Without tending to the core wounds and ideologies that underlie racialized oppression—indeed, any form of oppression—whatever structural changes we might win will be transient. To dismantle white supremacy a holistic transformation of both the social structures and the consciousness that sustains them is essential.

Simply understood, white supremacy is a system of economic, political, and social domination that enables white people—and particularly ruling class elites—to maintain power over everyone else. It is, in a sense, a sickness of the soul that diminishes the humanity of everybody it touches, including those who are its intended beneficiaries. But there is hope: because white supremacy is constructed, it can be deconstructed. I see this work as a spiritual imperative.

In the chapter on oneness and dualism we looked at the broader mechanisms of othering that divide us against one another. This chapter is a deeper examination of one of those mechanisms. Addressed primarily to my white-bodied kin, what follows is a "calling in" of sorts, inviting us into a lifelong commitment. There is a lot of information here. Most of us don't learn this history growing up, but knowledge has the power to awaken and motivate. Through understanding the history and costs of whiteness, we can better dedicate ourselves to the transgenerational project of liberation that is central to collective wholeness. I hope that this brief introduction to an urgent subject will hold something of value not only for white readers, but readers of every background, culture, and ethnicity.

Origins

My relationship to my own whiteness has, for most of my life, been an uneasy one. As the product of an interfaith marriage between a Jewish father and Christian mother, at times growing up I was ostracized and excluded from friendship groups for having Jewish heritage, and at others times for not being Jewish enough. I was repelled by the cruelty and arrogance in the behavior of many of my white peers toward anyone perceived as "other," echoing the dynamics of the larger society. In my 30s I dove into anti-racism work, critical race theory, and critical whiteness studies. I developed the political analysis, but my heart remained closed toward white people. And you can't truly understand something, let alone heal or transform it, from a place of disdain. In January 1996 I wrote to a friend:

> *Despite understanding the necessity to claim and address my own ancestry, I am ashamed of these kinfolk because of their whiteness. It's hard to write these words, to acknowledge my hypocrisy and all its implications.... Yet knowing that until I can embrace my white relations with an open heart I will always reject an essential and inescapable part of self, and my capacity to work for change will be hampered.*

It took another 15 years before I intentionally began to do the work that I had tried for so long to avoid—to heal my relationship to whiteness and soften my heart. But I held so many questions: What was it that caused white people to behave in ways so contradictory to Life? What allowed so many of us to be abusive toward other human beings, toward Nature and all creation? How did we get that way? Inquiry into what's behind someone's behavior—whether an individual or a group—can open the door to insight and even empathy. So often we cause harm out of unhealed wounds we may not even be aware of. Recognizing this does *not* excuse the harm, but it allows us to approach it in a different way, one more likely to facilitate change.

I began to explore my own ancestral lineage more intently than I had before; not just where each of my grandparents came from, but why they came and what their lives may have been like both in their home countries and as immigrants to the US. Their experiences were a lens into the lives of others. Many Europeans came to North America escaping something—religious or ethnic persecution, hunger, poverty, war, displacement. The journey over land and then by sea was long, dangerous, and costly. Like so many of today's immigrants, it was often a courageous choice of extremity made when the unknown dangers of the trip seemed preferable to the certain dangers of staying in place. Their stories included assimilation into whiteness and the insidious costs of that—a loss of connection to culture, language, and place and, for many, an existential feeling of unbelonging.[1]

Then I went back further in time, to look at the traumas experienced by the masses of European peasantry at the hands of empires seeking absolute domination over people and land. Especially ruthless was the persecution, extermination, and forced conversion of peoples on the European continent who practiced a Nature-based spirituality. Learning about the barbarity of the Inquisition, the witch burnings, and the Crusades helped me to view the consciousness we now call "whiteness" as a spiritual malformation, a dangerous malady in need of soul healing.

Resmaa Menakem, a psychotherapist and expert on racial trauma, points out that every torturous and horrific thing white-bodied people did (and do) to Black, Indigenous, and other people of color (who he refers to as "bodies of culture") we first did to other white people. He notes,

> During the Middle Ages in Europe, torture, mutilation, and other forms of savagery particularly on women were seen as normal aspects of life. Public executions were literally a spectator sport. As a result, when European "settlers" first came to this country centuries ago, they brought a millennium of inter-generational and historical trauma with them ... stored in the cells of their bodies.[2]

One of the ways human beings survive trauma is through numbing and disassociation. Is this what has so inured white people to the suffering of others, and allowed us to override our humanity to enact centuries of unimaginable cruelty? What began as the abuses of empire elites against the populous has been normalized in white culture as socially acceptable violence, persecution, and punishment. There is a lineage of ancestral trauma among people of European descent that must be addressed for racial justice and social transformation to be possible, and a reclamation of belonging to Earth and ancestors needed for the souls of white-identified people to heal.

The Invention of Whiteness

White supremacy has been part of the fabric of the US since its inception. We can make a distinction, however, between the *ideology* of whiteness that regards white-bodied European-descended people as inherently superior and entitled, and the biological condition of white-bodied-ness. The ideology is embedded in US culture, and we are steeped in it from birth, but it is not immutable. Part of the seduction strategy employed to keep white people enrolled in the system is the conveyance of certain social advantages. Things like self-determination, legal protection, presumption of innocence, and access to better education, healthcare, economic opportunity, and political representation. These should be universal rights equally held by all. Yet they are not. Their absence is not a lack of "privileges," or a sign of inferiority, but a systematic *denial of fundamental rights.*[3]

There is more than one way to be white, and we can choose to follow the example of white-bodied people who leveraged the access afforded by their whiteness to further the cause of racial justice. They were not simply allies and supporters, but true comrades who understood that systemic oppression harms everyone, and risked their lives in the struggle for liberation. They were abolitionists, members of the Communist Workers' Party, and organizers in the Southern Freedom Movement.

Most of their names are lost to history, but among the best known is Anne Braden. Born and raised in the Jim Crow South, she joined the Freedom Movement, working against racism, segregation, and white supremacy for nearly 60 years. Braden said, "Either you find a way to oppose the evil, or the evil becomes part of you and you are a part of it, and it winds itself around your soul like the arms of an octopus.... If I did not oppose it, I was ... responsible for its sins."[4] She affirmed that white people needed to fight racism as though our lives depended on it, because they do.

The history of white people working in solidarity with Black and other people of color in movements for justice is not taught in most of our schools. In fact, disruption of this multiracial alliance was the motivation for the invention of whiteness as a racialized identity. By connecting the dots through history, we can better understand and respond to the dynamics that we contend with today.

Prior to the late 1600s there were no "white people." Europeans were identified by their national ethnicities— English and French, Irish, German, or Dutch—and before that as Gaul, Saxon, Celtic, Norse, and so forth. Their lives were largely defined by the rigid categories of gender, religion, and position in the hierarchy of economic status and pedigree.

A legal contrivance of colonial capitalism, whiteness was used to consolidate wealth and power among one small subset of the population at the expense of others. It was strategically deployed to drive a wedge between white-bodied indentured servants and the Africans and Native Americans they lived and labored alongside, to prevent their joint uprising against the owning class minority. The token elevation of white workers was used to justify the permanent heritable enslavement of Africans, and create a perpetual source of unpaid labor.[5]

A series of 15th century papal bulls, known as the Doctrine of Discovery, provided religious and legal sanction for enslavement, colonization, and the extermination of the Indigenous population. The Doctrine permitted Christian Europeans to "discover" and lay claim to any lands not already inhabited by Christians, and to kill or enslave its "pagan" inhabitants.[6]

Pause for a moment here, and let that sink in. The impacts are devastating.

◎

As immigrants arrived to what is now the US, becoming "white" meant not only surrender of ethnic culture, but the surrender of ancestral traditions and the Indigenous spiritual lifeways of their homelands. All of us come from people who at one time lived in a primary relationship with the land. Some of us are further separated from that ancestral connection than others, but our relationship with beyond-human life doesn't cease just because we have forgotten. The land-based spirituality of pre-Christian Europe holds many similarities to that of Indigenous peoples everywhere. All are rooted in Nature and honor the sacred wholeness of Life.[7]

The suppression of Indigenous European spirituality is a violent erasure on its own, pre-dating trans-Atlantic immigration. Assimilation into Christian whiteness (whether by force or by choice) meant severing the power and belonging inherent in being grounded in a lineage of people and place. Perhaps this feeling of disconnection is part of what drives the callousness of white supremacy. Belonging confers a feeling of responsibility, accountability, and even love for who or what we belong to. It provides a sense of context and meaning.

It's helpful for white-bodied people to remember that the majority of our ancestors lived *before* white supremacy, before fracture from the Earth. We can reclaim our lost connections, call on those ancestors to guide and partner with us in the work of healing and liberation. I believe they are calling on us, in these times, to be the agents of repair, transforming the lineage of harm so that it will not continue to be perpetuated.

Facing the Pain: Acknowledging Truths

In Lee Mun Wah's 1994 documentary "The Color of Fear," a multi-racial group of men gather for a three-day retreat to explore issues of race.[8] There's a pivotal moment in which one of the white men is minimizing the experience of racism described by one of the African American men. Rather than contradict this denial, Lee quietly asks, "And what if the things he is telling you were true? What would that mean for you?"

Hearing this question, the white man breaks down in tears. He says, in essence, "I couldn't bear it." It would mean the world wasn't as he thought it was, that systematic oppression was in fact pervasive and devastating, and he wasn't the innocent "good guy" prospering by his own virtue that he imagined himself to be.

That degree of pain—both the pain of disillusionment, and the pain that is the lived experience of Black and other people of color in this country—can seem beyond bearing. Yet as white people we must be willing to go into this pain. To bear it. To feel it. To grieve it. To move through it and be changed by it. As with initiations, the only way out is through. Dismantling the fiction of whiteness to awaken our authentic souls is a crucial initiation for white people to undertake.

Going into the pain is like the fire of hell, but it is also the fire of purification, and of alchemy. However, we must be careful not to make *our* pain the center of attention, not to ask (implicitly or explicitly) for people of color to give up their rage or their grief to assuage our pain or ease our discomfort. That is *our* work as white-bodied people, *our* path to healing and maturity.

This is part of the intention behind the Truth and Reconciliation process—recounting and bearing witness to the crushing harms and injustice, and opening the way for repentance, reparation, and healing. At least this is the ideal. In actuality there has been more truth than reconciliation, but truth-telling must certainly precede reconcilement. And in many cases there is no previous relationship of mutual respect to return to, so "*re*-conciliation" is a misnomer. The process of healing takes time and work, and requires genuine accountability on the part of those who have enacted and benefitted from the harms.

Many people are familiar with the Truth and Reconciliation Commission (TRC) convened in South Africa in the wake of apartheid. TRCs have been held in the aftermath of other atrocities around the world, including the US. The Maine Wabanaki-State Child Welfare TRC (2013–2015) investigated the systematic removal of Wabanaki children from their families and tribal communities by the state, in a policy of cultural genocide. This placement of children with white foster and adoptive families followed on the heels of generations of Indigenous children in the US and Canada being abducted from their homes and sent to boarding schools where they were subjected to horrific abuses.[9]

Given the problematics of the term "reconciliation" in the context of 500 years of genocide, broken treaties, and stolen land, the Wabanaki TRC spoke instead of "Truth, Healing and Change." This feels like a more accurate depiction of both the process and intended outcomes for truth commissions in light of the historical reality in many of the settings where they are convened.

When I first learned about the Wabanaki TRC, it was heart rending. I had no idea of any personal connection with the Wabanaki people at the time, but recently I discovered that some of my maternal grandfather's ancestors, who immigrated from Northern Ireland in the 1700s, were among the early settlers in Wabanaki territory—in what is now New Brunswick, Canada. Although I don't know the specifics of their interactions, the history of settler colonialism provides context.

Discovering this forced a shift in my relationship to history. I felt more directly tied to the trespasses of colonization. I had taken some comfort in the fact that my immediate ancestors were recent arrivals in the US, even though—of course—I benefit from their assimilation into whiteness. I am embedded in the history of colonization, genocide, and enslavement simply through this. It is in me and I am in it, regardless. Yet these ancestors were part of the original harm, and that proximity felt like a more personal responsibility. I wanted to contribute in some way to the rematriation work in Wabanaki territory, returning the land to its sovereignty and the care of its original people, as a small step toward reparations. At first I thought these reparations were for me, but then I realized they were also for my ancestors. And that gave it a new level of importance.

As we saw in the chapter on healing across time, there's a way that the ancestors need us—here in the physical dimension—to help transform the traumas and abuses of the past. There is a healing that is only possible from within the human experience, and it is our calling to step into it as part of this turning of the age. In her book *Medicine Stories*, Aurora Levins Morales writes, "Acknowledging our ancestors' participation in the oppression of others . . . and deciding to balance the accounts on their behalf leads to greater integrity and less shame.... It becomes possible to see the choices we make right now as extensions of those inherited ones, and to choose more courageously as a result."[10]

Many people have affirmed the need for a US national truth commission on genocide and enslavement, to address the centuries-long impacts of these. The so-called "anti-woke" movement seeking to prevent any acknowledgment of the US history of enslavement, racial, and other forms of oppression is a strategic attempt to oppose the transformative power of reckoning with our past. But silencing a thing does not dispense with it, it only stifles the possibility of change. The truth-telling process is an opportunity to correct the historical record, documenting harms that have gone unaddressed. It intends to make both the perpetrators and general public aware of the full impacts of their actions, thus awakening the conscience—the humanity—of the offender and the nation, recognizing that these entities are often one and the same. Such awakening is a crucial step toward transformation.

Reconciliation is first reconciliation within oneself—no longer denying the harms we have perpetrated or permitted. Healing for the perpetrator is impossible without telling the truth to ourselves and to the witness of others. This truth-telling is not only central to grappling with large-scale harms, but can be engaged by each of us on the microscopic level of our individual daily interactions and mindset, allowing us to interrogate all the ways that whiteness shows up, and again and again to respond by making a different choice.

Reparations as a Sacred Practice

The Grassroots Reparations Initiative, a program of the Truth Telling Project, describes reparations as the midpoint between Truth and Reconciliation.[11] They believe reparations are a spiritual practice of healing moral and material harm, not merely a transactional event. As a matter of justice, the mandate for reparations to the descendants of kidnapped and enslaved Africans and to the descendants of the original peoples of the Americas is inarguable. However, there is also a deep repair needed for the souls of white people. The damage of centuries of white supremacy is carried in each of us (regardless of our political views and personal "woke-ness") and must be addressed. The simple fact that we, as white-bodied people, have benefitted from another's pain, from another's displacement and disenfranchisement, or even their death, is a soul wound that we carry.[12] If we recall the principle of tikkun—repair of the world and repair of the soul—we can understand reparations as an act of tikkun, a step toward the restoration of an original wholeness *for everyone.*

Reparations are not something that white-bodied people give Black, Indigenous, or other communities of color as a favor, or even a penance. Reparations are how *white people* get whole, how we get free. Reparations can be engaged not only as a necessary component of establishing economic justice, but as a collective ritual of remorse, grief, and amends . . . as a transformative spiritual act. A step toward healing.

Inner and outer transformation, as I've said, are not separate from one another; both are essential to genuine and lasting change.

Some people argue that the harms of slavery and genocide occurred too long ago to warrant compensation, but the epigenetics of trauma make it clear that even the *bodies* of Black and Indigenous people alive today are shaped by—and suffer from—the traumas of the past. Certainly, the social impacts of centuries of systematic oppression are an ongoing legacy. And the benefits conferred by a legacy of systematic advantage are alive in the bodies and circumstances of white people. But white people are also harmed by this system that divides the majority of humans against one another, struggling to preserve our little piece of safety while those at the top amass obscene wealth and power. The process of reparations can lead us to a broader social restructuring that fosters equity, and ultimately benefits everyone.

"Reparations must not be only an effort to compensate for past harms," writes theologian Kelly Brown Douglas, "they must also chart a pathway to a just future. Otherwise, reparations become little more than a salve for white guilt while the sin of white supremacy continues to thrive."[13] To repent, biblically speaking, is not just to feel remorse and contrition, but literally to turn and go in a different direction. In this sense, the repentance of white people is necessary—not just our guilt, shame, or regret, but to make a radical turn to a new way of being, living into an embodied anti-racist culture. Understanding how "whiteness" was constructed allows us to deconstruct it; understanding how it is legitimized and maintained, we can cease to legitimize and maintain it. This is the collective project of reorganizing an unjust society, centering the vision and leadership of the communities most impacted by generations of harm.

The Way Forward

The power of white supremacy and other forms of domination is neither inherent nor immutable. It is a result of subterfuge, manipulation, and deceit—and we can change it. True Power, inherent Power, is a spiritual quality residing in each of us, in Nature and in Life itself. How we invest that Power is up to us.

A key question to ask ourselves is, who we will be to our human and more-than-human siblings, and to the Earth: *other, ally, comrade, or kin?* Will we claim our belonging to the best of collective humanity and join the lineage of people working to dismantle supremacy in *all* its forms? Will we honor our oneness with all of Life and commit ourselves as agents of healing and transformation?

In an essay on liberative kinship, Pastor Nate Lee writes,

> There is nothing more threatening to white supremacy than the people realizing that their destinies are profoundly interlinked in their struggle against a racist economic order. We can call it allyship, we can call it being accomplices, but liberative kinship has always been at the heart of our communities, driving us toward a healing revolution that honors the complexity of our stories and the relationships that helped us survive. Liberative kinship means that we must learn to let go of all the ways we use a limited understanding of identity to build walls, to protect ourselves from the pain, suffering, and joy of others.[14]

As we find our way through the ravages of division and move toward collective wholeness, we can restore what was lost to many of us so long ago—our inherent belonging to Earth, ancestors, and the family of all creation. And we can choose to live in integrity with that belonging.

◎

REFLECTION PRACTICE

For white-bodied people:

I invite you into a deeper exploration on the lives of your ancestors before and after they became white. What were their home countries? Their cultures, languages, and spiritual traditions? If they came to the lands now known as the Americas, what were the circumstances by which they came? Were they considered "white" when they arrived? How did they become "white"? What did they give up in the process, and what did they gain? How were your ancestors complicit in colonization and/or the economy of enslavement? Did any of your ancestors work for liberation in partnership with people of color?

I invite you to also research the indigenous peoples of the lands your ancestors come from. Who were they and what were their lifeways before the imposition of empire and (if relevant) Christianization? Are any of those original people still living there today?

For everyone:

- *Was any of the information in this chapter new to you? If so, how does it shift your relationship to, or understanding of, whiteness?*
- *What cultural and spiritual practices from your ancestral lineage were part of your own upbringing? How much has been lost and what were the circumstances of that loss? Have you done anything to reclaim some of those practices, foods, languages, traditions, etc.?*
- *What are the migration stories of your ancestors? Was their migration forced or by choice? What were their lives like before, during, and after?*
- *Have any of your ancestors worked cross-racially for liberation? Perhaps for the abolition of slavery, in the labor movement, in communist or socialist organizations, or in the Southern Freedom, Farm Workers, anti-war, or other movements?*
- *You may wish to write a letter to one or more of your ancestors . . . and perhaps to write a letter from them back to you.*

PART FOUR

A Wider Belonging

*Honoring our kinship with one another and
all expressions of Life.*

We are a part of everything that is beneath us, above us, and around us. Our past is our present, our present is our future, and our future is seven generations past and present.

—Winona LaDuke

Everything on the planet that is part of life and that sustains life is an ancestor.

—Vandana Shiva

I want to be an ancestor who nourished legacies of health without forgetting the pain. I want to be remembered as someone who helped create space to nurture a sense of belonging, belonging to that fundamental fabric of wholeness that ultimately created us and will absorb us once again.

—Melissa K. Nelson

10
Life, Death, Ancestors &
Coming Generations

EACH OF US IS WOVEN INTO THE FABRIC of life in relationship with generations past, present, and future. We can be intentional about these relationships: cultivating our kinship with Nature, connecting with people younger and older than ourselves, and seeking communion with the ancestors and the yet-to-be-born. Quite literally, we are the ancestors of the coming generations.

Attuning to these relationships evokes a sense of responsibility, obligation, and concern. It demands we think beyond the narrow margins of our own particular life or season. Because the US is a relatively young culture, we can be myopic in our focus on immediate gratification and individual self-advancement leading, in part, to the harrowing conditions we now face. We would do well to learn from the long view of cultures much older than our own. When we feel ourselves as part of a longer trajectory of time and a larger circle of belonging, it invites a practice of intergenerational accountability—not only to our human descendants, but to all of life. In his poem "hieroglyphic stairway," Drew Dellinger echoes this concern, writing *"it's 3:23 in the morning / and I can't sleep / because my great great grandchildren / ask me in dreams / what did you do while the Earth was unravelling?"*[1]

There is so much possibility in this moment—for good or for harm. This is an amazing time to be alive on the planet. Terrifying and painful, yes, and also pivotal. The choices we make will have repercussions for generations to come. How will we be accountable to the web of Life and to the great great grandchildren who whisper in our dreaming?

Robin Wall Kimmerer, a plant ecologist and author from the Citizen Potawatomi Nation, writes of a particular Grandmother Maple tree she visits for counsel, and shares what she learned. "To be a good ancestor," Grandmother taught her, "you have to build good soil."[2] In this lies the potential for regeneration after hardship. Kimmerer recalls the volcanic eruption of Mount St. Helens, and how in the wake of so much devastation, new life gradually emerged in small pockets of good soil. Good soil holds both the composted nourishment from the past and the seeds and spores of future life, deposited by wind or birds or animals. These are the resources that support a future we "cannot imagine, but trust will arise."[3] The maple is a very generous ancestor, Kimmerer explains. In autumn some trees withdraw all their nutrients inward to be used the following year, before dropping their leaves. Those leaves contain little to feed the soil. But maples, she says, hold nothing back. They offer their leaves full of rich nutrients to the ecosystem of the Earth, making wonderful soil. They give all that is within them to nourish the flourishing of future life.

As I read Kimmerer's words, I was reminded of a weekend-long gathering I participated in some years ago with a circle of wise and beautiful souls. Among those present was Bernice Johnson Reagon, Freedom Singer, scholar, activist, and founder of the vocal ensemble Sweet Honey in the Rock. I will always remember her saying that she wanted to live so fully, to give everything that was in her to give, so that when she died the only thing left would be an empty husk. As she spoke, something within me leapt to attention: *I want to live that way, too.* Maybe it resonates with you as well? Like a touchstone to keep in our pocket that calls us back to what's important. (Remember, the most *urgent* thing before us is not always the most *important*.)

As we talk about giving all that is ours to give, about living with meaning and purpose through times of upheaval, death can be a powerful ally. Death is, of course, the portal through which we enter the ancestor realm at the end of our human incarnation, but it can also be a worthy companion in our life now. It helps us clarify our values, and offers a compass (and a motivation!) that can guide our way.

Death as Ally

In the movie *Defending Your Life*, Meryl Streep's character sits in a darkened room—part movie theater, part courtroom—with her defense attorney, the prosecution, and a handful of others. Streep has died and this is her life review, part of the formal proceedings to determine where she will go from here. Projected on the screen we see a suburban house late at night, engulfed in flames. We watch as Streep wakes her sleeping children and carries them out of the house to safety. Cheering neighbors line the street. Then the youngest child realizes the family's beloved cat is still trapped inside. Streep rushes back into the burning house to rescue the cat. Some tense moments later, she emerges through the smoke with the cat cradled in her arms. The audience in the courtroom wipes tears from their eyes as Streep smiles contentedly at the memory. She has lived an exemplary life.

The scene then shifts to another courtroom theater, where we see film clips from the life of the character played by Albert Brooks. They highlight the many times he acted out of fear, falling short of his best possibilities and denying what he knew in his heart was right.

The idea of a "life review" process that takes place upon our death has found its way from spiritual traditions into popular culture through movies such as *Defending Your Life* and *Heart and Souls*. Sometimes the protagonist is offered an opportunity to go back into the human world to mend the harms they caused and correct the things they wish they had done differently. In movies it's often a humorous portrayal, but the idea is a serious one. I don't believe in a judgmental deity waiting to mete out punishment or reward, but I do believe that we are given the opportunity to reflect on and learn from our experience after we leave this life.

Consider what your "film clips" would look like. When the time comes for your life review, what do you imagine you'll feel about the scenes you see? What are the scenes that will bring you the most satisfaction? And what (if anything) will you wish you could amend?

Perhaps a better question is, what do you *want* to see, to remember, to celebrate when your time comes? How can you live *now* in order for that to become the "movie" of your life review? What is one small step in that direction you can take right now? Follow it with another. And continue in that direction so you'll feel satisfied at the end that you gave the entirety of your gifts.

Living with chronic illness, and having several times been close to death, imagining this life review has become a helpful instrument of discernment, a measure by which I am guided on my path. I ask, "If I die without doing _____, will I regret it?" (My regrets have always been more about things I didn't do than things I did.) In times of decision, this clarifying question has been my litmus test, especially regarding profession and purpose.

The dominant culture in the US teaches us to fear death, to avoid and deny it at all costs. However, many people around the world view death differently. They understand that death is an ally, a friend that walks with us throughout our human journey and ushers us across the threshold into larger Life at the journey's end. Death can also usher us into the experience of larger Life *during* our earthly sojourn, sometimes through the invitation of our spiritual practice, and sometimes surprising us, coming unbidden. This is another face of the mystic encounter: breaking open our narrow identity to feel an expanded oneness with all that is, as we die to the sense of separation.

Death is integral to the archetype of apocalypse, the necessary prerequisite for rebirth and regeneration to follow. Death is how things transform. Earlier, I wrote about the process of initiation as a kind of death; and death itself is also an initiation. Indeed, every loss we suffer is a death to what was: the end of a job or relationship, a change in health status, a betrayal of trust, the shifting identity of different seasons in our lives. There is the death of illusions, dying to old beliefs to behold a deeper truth. With each of these deaths, each shedding and releasing, we have the potential to emerge more free and more true—closer to our essential nature.

A saying of the Prophet Muhammad counsels, "Die before you die." Omid Safi, a respected Islamic scholar with a gentle mystic's soul, explains the "two deaths" in the teaching of the Prophet this way: the first is the death of the ego, surrendering the small self to the Divine, the second is the death of the body. Everyone, he points out, will encounter the second, but not everyone will experience the first. For those who do, a more luminous and fulfilling human life lies in between those two deaths. Safi writes, "'Die before you die' means this: live the way that you would if you had two hours to live. Live in love, live in gratitude. Tell, show, be in love.... Leave nothing unsaid, undone."[4]

"Death is but the middle of a long life," one Celtic proverb states.[5] Death of the body—the ending of our human incarnation—takes place within the larger Life of our spiritual existence, but does not end it. Birth and death and the (small-L) life they bookend define a brief span within the eternality of (capital-L) Life. This has been referred to by several authors as "a parenthesis in eternity."[6] When I describe this concept in the classroom, I draw a long line with an arrow at each end to signify Life, and then mark a small segment of that within the bounds of parentheses to represent the span of a single incarnation. Those who believe in reincarnation might put multiple sets of parentheses on that line.

Because Life is nonlinear and multidimensional, not only does our existence extend beyond the chronological duration of our human years, it extends beyond our human experience even as we inhabit that experience. Here again is the mystic intuition of moving outside the constraints of the finite egoic self into an expanded awareness of the larger Life that encompasses all. How does that shift in perspective change our relationship with death ... and with life—our individual experience of living, our choices and priorities?

Howard Thurman taught that "a good death is made up of the same elements as a good life."[7] When we find meaning and purpose beyond the confines of our individualized existence, seeing ourselves as part of the purposes of larger Life, it is, he said, "this *beyond dimension* that saves the individual life from being swallowed by the tyranny of present needs, present hungers, and present threats."[8] If we are terrified of death, then the mere threat of it controls us. Releasing this fear frees us to more fully and boldly experience *life*, to discover the exhilarating territory beyond our comfort zone and find the magic there. Anchored in the Life that is unconstrained by the boundaries of human birth and death, we are empowered to explore and express the full measure of our being, to live into our purpose in a rapidly transforming world. Thurman said, "The time and the place of a man's life is the time and place of his body, but the meaning of a man's life is as eternal and as significant as with all of him he *wills* to make it."[9]

How would you shape your life if you had only a few years left in this body? How would you live if you were not afraid? Is something pulling at you? Perhaps a vision of how you are called to live that feels beyond your capacity or stirs up resistance . . . yet is something you know in your bones is yours to do, to be. What is holding you back? Or as Dr. Thurman might ask, what is holding you back . . . *really*?

As I come to these questions repeatedly in my own life, I find that most of what holds me back is myself. It's so easy to get seduced by the million competing demands for our time and attention. It takes discipline to call ourselves into purpose, again and again and again, until at last it becomes our habitation. In this way, the companionship of death is another medicine of the soul, summoning us to the fullness of our gifts.

Becoming a Good Ancestor

One of the best things about being in one's 60s, where I find myself now, is the feeling of connection to generations. Our children (by birth or otherwise) are grown. They have children, and maybe even grandchildren, most of them known and dear. There is still a living generation older than we are who remain on the planet as our elders. And there are generations we have known and loved who are now ancestors. The relationships are visceral, proximate. I have physically touched these beloveds, two or even three generations in either direction, and they offer a bridge to those long before and yet to come. It's a tangible relationship across time, a weaving into life in a way that is intimate and precious.

When Zulu *sangoma* (shaman and healer) Baba Vusamazulu Credo Mutwa said "We must think like grandmothers," I expect this is part of it.[10] The unconditional love, the patience and selflessness of grandmothers, yes, but also our primary connection to so many generations of beings. And the insight that comes with having lived for more than a while.

You don't have to be any particular age or gender to think like a grandmother. I've known some younger folks and some masculine-gendered folks who carry the grandmother spirit. And I've known some biological grandmothers who don't. If we take Baba Mutwa's counsel and embrace this as spiritual practice, how does thinking like grandmothers invite us to live? I like to imagine the world that would create—one shaped by wisdom, that honors the Earth and all living beings. One that is steeped in the kind of fierce love that doesn't put up with a bunch of mess. One that calls everyone up to the full expression of their genius. The grandmother spirit thinks beyond her own lifespan and plants trees (both literal and metaphorical) to nourish future generations, trees that will reach maturity long after she is gone. This spirit leads us to be courageous in working for peace and fighting injustice. It is the midwife who knows how to heal, and how to support those who are birthing babies, ideas, and worlds.

Practicing this grandmother spirit is excellent preparation for being a good ancestor when we leave the physical life. This is how we become the "good soil" that Robin Wall Kimmerer's Grandmother Maple encouraged. Being a good ancestor is not about how we will someday be remembered, but about how we live *now*. We are shaping the collective future by our decisions and actions every breathing moment.

A surprising number of younger people are concerned with how to become a good ancestor, and making it a guidepost for their lives. Author Layla F. Saad hosted the Good Ancestor podcast and had a popular blog and Instagram account on the topic. Her audience is mostly millennials, like she is. In her blog, Saad writes,

> Becoming a good ancestor is something that we actually have to practice in our everyday lives.... It is something that we use as a north star to guide us on whether or not we want to spend time on a certain activity, opportunity, creation, or even relationship. It's a filter that we can use to see ourselves in the world, and how we choose to interact with the world.[11]

Like so much else we have spoken of in this book, there are both inward and outward dimensions to becoming a good ancestor. Embodying our soul's purpose, the healing we do on personal and inherited trauma, deepening our communion with the Sacred, the work of forgiveness and reconciling relationships, all these help us turn our wounds into wisdom to serve coming generations. Alongside this, our commitment to social justice, transformation, and collective liberation, to honoring the Earth and all of life, shifts the foundations of the world our children's children will inhabit. All this, of course, is a direction not a destination. This is not an assignment we will ever complete; nevertheless it is one for us to pursue with integrity.

Calling on Our Spiritual Ancestors

The responsibility we have to past and future generations can feel a bit daunting, but in healthy relationships responsibility is reciprocal, as is care. There is tremendous love and wisdom available to us beyond the dimension of the mundane world. I want to share some practical ways to tap into that potent energy.

In a previous chapter, I offered practices for working with ancestors in your own lineage. In addition to the ancestors in our bloodline, we also have cultural and spiritual ancestors. Who do you strive to emulate, or look to for inspiration? It might be a teacher or mentor who encouraged you in life, or an historical figure you never met but whose spirit you resonate with. Come to them with humility and respect, ask for their guidance, and cultivate the relationship. I believe this is literally possible: that other dimensions exist and we can be in relationship with them. Still, even if you don't believe this, you can use your imagination to connect with the essence of a person and look to their example for direction. Evoke, for instance, the creative excellence of Maya Angelou or Frida Kahlo to ignite your own. Or reach to the socially engaged mystics to guide your activism.

The Elements—Air, Fire, Water, Earth—are also our ancestors, as are the stars and everything in Nature. Physically, we are made from their substance; spiritually we are shaped by their essence and qualities. (Just pause and feel that for a moment. How does it shift your self-perception, your sense of belonging and empowerment, to know you are the progeny of these mighty forces?) We can turn to them for insight, healing, and support. Many traditions, including Celtic spirituality, Jewish mysticism, and the Indigenous wisdom shared by Brother Tetteh and others, include teachings about the Elements. The Spirit of the Air is the life-giver, bringer of fresh possibilities. The Spirit of the Fires is the sacred alchemy of transformation and transmutation. The Spirit of the Waters is the cleansing, purifying, restorative energy. The Spirit of the Earth is the power of bonding, nurturing, stabilizing love. Develop your relationship with each of them—physically and spiritually—and invite them into your prayers and meditations.

An effective way to connect with each of these energies we have spoken of—ancestors, coming generations, the Elements, and Nature—is through the breath.

In the quiet of your meditations, imagine your ancestors standing supportively behind you. Visualize them, generation upon generation. You may want to include your non-biological ancestors as well. Inhale deeply, breathing love and blessing intention back into the generations, and as you exhale feel their love (or wisdom, strength, courage, etc.) breathing itself forward into you, infusing you. Doing this regularly will help cultivate your ancestral connections and bring life to your relationship with them.

Similarly, you can breathe into the vitality and vision of the coming generations. In the fluidity of time we are in relationship with the yet-to-be-born generations *now*, and can seek their counsel just as we do with our ancestors. These future generations inhabit a world on the other side of apocalypse. What can they see and understand that is beyond our imagining? What do they want us to know? I pray often for their guidance and send them my blessings. Again, these relationships are not limited to blood lineage. Whether we have parented or not, we all have children, grandchildren, and generations to whom we are accountable.

We belong to a vast kinship with dimensions seen and unseen that extend across the bounds of time. We can draw on the energies of an oak tree or a mountain to amplify our strength and stability. Or we can breathe in the majesty of the galaxies, and pour their vibrance into our body–mind–being. When doing this, I feel a profound sense of peace. During some of the most difficult times in my journey with chronic illness, this became a regular part of my practice and gifted me with relief from the pain. Indeed, we can commune with any aspect of Life because, in the mystic understanding, we are one with everything and everyone.

Through this oneness, we can also direct beneficial energy where it is needed to people, communities, historical moments, places, and Elements—partnering in the collective project of human and planetary transformation in these swiftly changing times. There are no limits. We are fractal parts of an infinite Wholeness and can touch any aspect of that Whole. These practices also work against the feelings of separation that underlie the dualistic worldview, and the fractured world it creates. Consciously cultivating our felt connection with Nature, ancestors, and coming generations fosters a sense of belonging to these precious relations that is at once healing and empowering.

---◎---

REFLECTION PRACTICE

Death is the threshold we cross to enter the ancestral realm. In these times when so much is dying, it can be a powerful ally in crafting a life of meaning. We can use contemplation of our imagined death to explore our values, purpose, relationships, and priorities, and to highlight the people and things we hold most precious. For now, let's revisit some of the reflection questions on death and dying from this chapter. I invite you to journal on the following:

- *Imagine your "life review" process. Looking back over your incarnation at the time of your death, how will you feel about what you see? What will bring you the most satisfaction, and what (if anything) will you wish you could amend?*

- *In a more proactive sense, what do you want to see, to remember, to celebrate when your time comes? How do you need to live now in order for that to become the "movie" of your life review? What steps can you take in that direction beginning now?*

- *Is there something pulling at you that you know in your bones is yours to do, to be? Perhaps a vision of how you are called to live that feels beyond your capacity or stirs up resistance? How would you live if you were not afraid? And what is holding you back ... really?*

- *How would you shape your life if you had only a few years left in this body? A few months? A few weeks? What would you do differently? How can this awareness become a guide to enrich your life now, however long it may be?*

- *What changes can you make in your life now in order to be a good ancestor to those who will follow? A good relative to Life in all its many expressions?*

How can we listen across species, across extinction, across harm? ... Listening is not only about the normative ability to hear, it is a transformative and revolutionary resource that requires quieting down and tuning in.

—Alexis Pauline Gumbs

Deep listening is an act of surrender. We risk being changed by what we hear.... Listening is how we gain the information we need to reimagine.

—Valarie Kaur

The language of emergence is listening, allowing oneself to always be moved and changed, tuning into the wisdom that is beyond words and language.

—Kerri Kelly

◎

11

Deep Listening

CULTIVATING THE CAPACITY FOR DEEP LISTENING is essential as we find our way through the wilderness of convergent crises. As a planetary community, we are in a liminal space of collective unknowing. Conjecture, predictions, hope, and pessimism abound, but in truth we don't know if humanity will survive or what life on the planet will look like if we do.[1] *We must listen.* Spirit speaks to us through the loving breath of Earth, the many intelligences of Nature, the whispering of ancestors and coming generations, the knowing in our bones.

Deep Listening encompasses mindful compassionate attention to the world around us: to ourselves, our bodies, our own suffering and need, as well as to the suffering and needs of others and the Earth. Listening as a practice of healing; not to judge or criticize, but with the intention of connection. Such listening evokes a profound and reverent sensitivity to what lies beneath the surface. A simultaneous reaching out and receptivity from the belly of being, alert for the scent of what is behind, below, above, between the words spoken, the actions taken. Listening as a spiritual discipline. Listening to gesture, breath and tone, to passion and to grieving and to laughter, to hunger, to terror, rage, and grace. Listening for the "sound familiar" within a stranger's voice.

During my training in clinical medicine we learned to attune our diagnostic ear to the inner chambers of the heart, to perceive the subtlest rumble or rub, to describe and even imitate the whisper-soft murmurs and whooshes of the body's coded language. At first it was an exercise in frustration, but then somehow, with patience and persistence, a new ear was opened—one that was able to decipher the code. I am reminded of this when my acupuncturist places her fingers on my wrist to read my pulses. It's more like a listening than a touch, as if there are special ears in each of her fingertips that "hear" the quality of *chi* the way I listened for the character of my patients' heartbeat.

Now I strive to listen with that same acuity to the hearts of those who come to me for counseling and prayer . . . to attend to the diagnostic murmurs and rumbles of an often-brokenhearted world. At the same time, I seek to hone my listening to discern the hum of divine connectivity within all of Life . . . to place my careful fingers so tenderly on the pulsebeat of Being that I sense even the rustling portents of its dreaming. This is listening with the mystic's ear that recognizes the hearer and the heard are one, both part of that infinite creative Is-ness that imagined them into expression.

To listen from this place requires the cultivation of silence. As theologian Dorothee Soelle described it, "the silence of the mouth, the silence of the mind, the silence of the will."[2] Through this practice, and through the intention of spiritual availability, the third ear begins to open. In silence is the spaciousness to listen deeply, to offer the fullness of our presence in service to the revelation of another's wholeness. This communion is found not only in our encounters with other humans, but through our reverent listening to the world—to Earth herself, and to the voices of her many children.

In our high-tech society, we are constantly bombarded with information, with sensory inputs, sound, and noise. We carry our computers in our hand, eyes glued to tiny screens, ears assaulted by a fast-paced cacophony both within and without. A 24-hour news cycle keeps us constantly on edge, anticipating the latest terror or tragedy. All this takes a heavy toll on our physical, mental, and spiritual well-being. How can we hear the soundless voice of the deep? And how might our lives, and the world we create, be different if we explored a deeper listening? Poet Mark Nepo says, "When lost, we simply have to remember to put our ear to the earth, or to our heart, and we will hear a warmth that guides."[3] Imagine doing that. What would you hear? . . . How would it change you?

Listening Within

We can open to a wisdom greater than our own for insight, seeking clarity and direction beyond our logical mind. Like any discipline, this kind of consecrated listening takes practice. It requires we inhabit the place of not-knowing, living into a question rather than hastening to answer it. Ranier Maria Rilke, in his *Letters to a Young Poet*, counsels his young correspondent to "love the questions."[4] The great agriculturalist, inventor, and mystic George Washington Carver believed if you love something enough, it will reveal its secrets to you.[5] Love the questions, live into them, and remain alert for their whispered revelations.

In my classes on spiritual formation, I include a unit on discernment. It's a term widely used in religious circles, but variably understood. Discernment is a practice of dedicated listening and patient receptivity. Prepare by emptying yourself—as much as you can—of all the static that filters, blocks, or confuses: releasing your fears and desires, attachments and agendas. Pouring all of it out through tears, words, body and breath, so you can enter into a space of unknowing. Listening with belly and bones. Then keep emptying, keep opening and listening ... faithfully. For as long as it takes. Eventually something will arise in you. Not in your mind. Somewhere deeper, below the level of thought. An intuitive sense. At first it may be almost imperceptible, just a hint of a direction in which to proceed. Trust it. Follow it. See what unfolds ... without assumptions or expectations. Intentionally practicing curiosity will help you stay open.

Keep walking with the question—making it your companion—step by step, as you are guided. Sometimes things might look a certain way for a while and then shift, and shift again. Like in a treasure hunt where you don't get the map to the treasure from your starting point. You just get the clue to the next place, and there find the clue to the one after that, and from there the next after that. Along the way we are changed. This is how Life works. We must keep listening always. Like using a GPS navigation system, we need to be attentive to constant updates and recalibrations as the conditions around us evolve.

Living in not-knowing is different from living in confusion. It's a state of curiosity, presence, receptivity, and equanimity. Of beginner's mind. Our job—our *discipline*—is to get our own thinking mind out of the way and expand our availability to that Spirit within, the Knower, so it can guide us. But as long as *we* think we know, there is no opening for a wisdom beyond ours to get a message through.

Sometimes guidance comes in a dream, or several people will all "happen" to mention the same book. Nature may offer a teaching, or our own body will give us a sign. Our language has remnants of the body as oracle. When we say "I have a gut feeling," "it gave me goosebumps," "it took my breath away," or "that's a pain in the neck"—it's information. Last weekend I was looking at something off to the side as I headed toward my car, and walked smack into a traffic sign. Hard. It was so bizarre that I asked, "Okay, what's the message?" And instantly I got, "Focus on where you want to go." It was 100% apt advice for something I've been wrestling with. Although I prefer my messages without a lump on my head, it certainly got—and has kept—my attention! How often have you thought, "something told me." Who or what is that "something" and how can you listen to it more? A pastor I know says "Something" is one of God's many names.

Of course there are other voices that might masquerade as truth—the inner critic, the internalized abuser, cultural expectations, our own desires and aversions. It takes time to begin to recognize which voice is speaking, to become familiar enough with the "sound" of Inner Wisdom that your bones know when it is the source of the message. If a message belittles you, shames you, or is cruel in any way—that's not it. Recognition of the true is like a spiritual muscle we develop through the consistent exercise of discernment. Many of us wait until The Most Important Decision of Our Life to reach for discernment, but instead make it a way of living. Musicians and athletes don't just jump in on the night of the concert or the big game, they practice all the time in order to be ready *whenever* they are called upon. Practice being in relationship with your Inner Knower until you recognize its energetic signature and it becomes the reliable presence of an intimate friend.

We use the term "listening," and I have been speaking mostly in auditory terms, but I don't actually hear anything in discernment. Some people do. Other people see images. I get an intuitive communication, a direct transmission of information. Sometimes it comes in the linearity of language, and sometimes as a composite or metaphorical understanding that I then have to unwind into words. It's so subtle that for many years I discounted it, and then—almost as an experiment—I asked, what if this is guidance? What if I follow it? The more I did, the stronger that muscle of recognition grew. Now it is as familiar as my own breath, I trust it and am continually benefitted by its counsel. This is what I mean by practice. When the moment of The Big Decision arises, you will already have a well-worn trail to follow. As you explore this kind of inner listening, and some of the practices below, you'll begin to discover the ways that Guidance reveals itself to you.

Asking Generative Questions

Journaling was a helpful bridge in cultivating this listening process. I could tell when it was me writing and when that "Something" was offering insight. Eventually I was able to tune in and receive the communication without the need for pen and paper. But from time to time I still turn to journaling, or Spirit will just chime in with a message when I am writing.

Sometimes I go for a walk with a question I am carrying, to talk it over with my wise friend within, and use the voice memo app on my phone to record the insights that come as we consider it together. Or I take a question to bed with me, asking for the morning to bring greater understanding. You'll find what works best for you to hear the language of your own soul.

The kind of question we ask is key. For instance, the question "what's wrong with me?" is less generative than "what are some ways I could approach this differently?" Each brings a different type of answer. The first yields a list of personal shortcomings; the second, a list of creative solutions. The same is true of questions for our collective life. In medicine for example, if instead of asking how we can kill cancer cells, we asked how we can restore those cells to wholeness—what a different style of medicine we would have. In the realm of social justice work, abolitionists advocate that instead of asking how we can stop people from committing whatever the offense may be, by policing or incarceration, we ask instead *why* someone is engaging in that behavior, and address the cause. We may determine the cause to be poverty, mental illness, unhealed trauma. Questions set the course for our direction in inquiry and thus in life. The quality of our lives is directly informed by the questions we ask. With practice, we can learn to ask generative questions.

There's another method for seeking guidance I teach in my classes: that of listening through Nature, consulting the natural world as an oracle. Ideally, you can do this outdoors, physically present with Nature's expressions. Even if you are in an urban area, maybe there's a park or garden you can go to. If not, you can turn within to connect with Nature through your imagination.

To begin, take a clean sheet of paper, or use your journal, and write your question at the top of the page. You may want to re-read the paragraph above about choosing a generative question. Sometimes a question can simply be: *what do I need to know right now?* Once you've written the question, center yourself in meditation, taking a few slow deep breaths and quieting the chatter in your mind. Offer a prayer welcoming only that which is of the highest integrity, and asking to be guided to the message the natural world has for you. It may be the response to your question comes from a tree, an insect, an animal, a stone, the wind, or the sun. Something large or small. Everything in Nature is alive and has intelligence. Don't use your mind to figure it out, just be open to where your consecrated attention is called. Then, with humility, ask that entity to share its message.

You can act as the scribe, allowing the messenger to write through your pen and onto the page. Or you might record the message as a voice memo on your phone, or whatever works best for you. When it feels like the communication is complete, ask your messenger any clarifying questions you have, or engage them in dialogue. To conclude your session, thank them for what they shared and offer your blessing.

Listening Together

Sometimes the most helpful guidance comes not through answers, but from good questions. In the Quaker tradition there is a formal method for exactly that practice of sacred querying, used in a group setting called the clearness committee. Dating back to the 1660s, it was first used as a process for weighing decisions in the life of the Meeting (the Quaker spiritual community or congregation). In contemporary times, a clearness committee—or clearness circle—is convened to support an individual's process of discernment as they seek clarity on a major life decision or are struggling with a specific problem.

In a clearness circle no advice is given, no commiseration shared. The practice is strictly about sacred and attentive listening, and the offering of honest open questions. These "evoking questions" are designed to help the focus person attune to the deeper knowing that lies within them, the wisdom of their soul. The questions asked are brief and authentic—not thinly veiled assumptions, judgments, or counsel. A period of silence follows each question and each response, allowing space for reflection. The focus person can choose to pass on any question. The entire process is confidential; participants will not speak to others about what was said, nor will they speak about it with the focus person afterward, unless specifically invited by them to do so.

Parker Palmer is a writer, teacher, activist, and Quaker who has used the clearness process for many decades in his own life and work. He explains that Quakers believe "our guidance comes not from an external authority but from the inner teacher, and we need community to help us clarify and amplify the inner teacher's voice."[6] The goal of the committee is not "to fix the focus person," Palmer notes, "so there should be no sense of letdown if the focus person does not have [their] problems 'solved' when the process ends. A good clearness process does not end—it keeps working within the focus person long after the meeting is over."[7] Palmer's book, *A Hidden Wholeness*, includes more detailed guidelines for convening a clearness committee, if this is a practice you wish to engage. (A link to download these guidelines is in the endnotes.)

Another form of listening together is what in the Celtic tradition is called the *anam cara* or soul friend. My version of this has been what I refer to as a "spiritual jogging partner." Though I'm not a runner, the metaphor of jogging together is apt. Rev. Deborah L. Johnson and I have been spiritual comrades on life's road for more than 30 years. We pray together, encourage and challenge each other, vent and confide, offer reflection, celebrate victories, and both witness and foster one another's growth. When I suggested the term spiritual jogging partner to her years ago, what I meant by it was a spiritual companion, committed to our own and our partner's evolution. Someone to provide accountability and motivation when we fall off our practice, and to inspire us in becoming our best selves. Who is sagging and who is motivating would likely switch back and forth a lot, but that was the point: one of us would always be there to say "you can do this, let's go!" Indeed, this is what we have become for one another.

What has been surprising is how much our journeys each mirror the other's. The particulars of the situations we are navigating might be different, but the dynamics have been remarkably parallel—especially the spiritual "lessons" about things like leadership, surrender, and releasing attachment. Thus, we learn not only from our own experience, but through one another's, and our prayers are very often one-size-fits-both. Since each of us is personally and professionally someone people turn to when they need support, it's wonderful to have a genuinely reciprocal relationship with a friend who sees, knows, loves, and respects us, but won't let us get away with bullshit. We were in our 30s when we first met, and we are now in our 60s. Just that shared witness of each other's development over time is a gift, and the number of prayers we have prayed together along the way is astounding to consider.

The Inner Sanctuary

Prayer is foundational to so many traditions, and can be practiced in myriad ways. We can think of prayer as a movement in consciousness to bring us—the one praying—into alignment with the Divine. Our prayer doesn't change God (or the Universe, Spirit, etc.), it changes *us*. Howard Thurman said that through prayer *we* are answered and the hunger of our heart is fed, regardless of what does or doesn't happen with the situation we are praying about.[8]

When we understand this, it allows us to explore prayer beyond the confines of a particular religious formula or personal convention. In my classes on spiritual formation, I begin the session on prayer by inviting students to quickly list ten prayer methods that they have experienced. Next, I ask them to list the ways they commune with the Divine, refresh their souls, or honor the holy in their lives. The point of the exercise is not the specific things on their lists, but to illustrate something. People usually struggle to come up with ten responses for the list of prayer methods, while the second set of responses—about communion with the Sacred—comes much more easily. If we release prayer from the narrow box where we may have placed it, we discover that anything that aligns us with the Sacred Presence can be seen as prayer.

Some people have negative associations with prayer based on past religious experience. If that's the case for you, please don't let it keep you from finding your own unique language of communion with Larger Life. I had a student who painted her prayers, creating a watercolor and mixed media collage in response to whatever crisis was in the news headlines, and incorporating a vision for healing. I know people who drum their prayers, or dance them. I sometimes walk my prayers into the Earth with each intentional step, or plant them like seeds in the soil of my garden. When my prayers are about releasing something, I use the practice of weeding to pull what I need to let go of out from the root, or take a shower to wash clear of thought patterns or emotions that no longer serve. Sometimes I sing my heart in prayerful longing, devotion, affirmation, or gratitude. There are no limits to how we pray.

Prayer is at least as much about where we pray *from* as where we pray *to*. I begin by anchoring myself in the larger Life of Source: the power of the Elements, the wisdom of the ancestors, the vision and possibility of the yet-to-be-born generations, the infinite majesty of stars and galaxies, the potency of the *Ruach*—that first creative breath of the Divine upon the "Darkness of the Deep" that sparked manifestation into form. When I enter into oneness with all of this, it is no longer just "little me" petitioning some reluctant external deity, but a power and a word greater than myself that takes over. I have the sense of *being prayed* rather than "driving" the prayer. These are often declarative or blessing prayers, rather than beseeching ones.[9] Yet there are times when I am struggling and it is "little me" that can only muster a call for help. That too is prayer.

I was very moved when I read these words by Archbishop Desmond Tutu: "There are times, many times, when I can't pray, I am too tired to pray or I am experiencing a darkness of the soul. All I can do is be in the presence of God and say, 'All I can give you is me on my knees,' and throw myself into the stream of worship. And there I am immersed in the adoration and the love of God."[10]

In one of Howard Thurman's lectures he quotes a passage from Olive Schreiner's novel, *The Story of an African Farm*. When asked, "Do you ever pray?" one of the characters gives this striking reply: "No, I never do. But I'll tell you where I could pray: If there was a wall of rock on the edge of a world, and one rock stretched out far into space, and I stood alone on that rock, alone, with stars above me and stars below. I would not say anything, but the feeling would be prayer."[11] I encourage you to explore where and how you experience the expansiveness of that feeling in your own life, and *cultivate that*.

Some things can only be expressed in silence, in a wordless movement of the heart. More and more often I find myself praying in this wordless empty-fullness and full-emptiness of simultaneous yearning and completion . . . this bursting urgency and perfect peace . . . the communion of Silence. Prayer can become a climate we lean into; it can become our habitation. Being present with the deepest parts of myself to that which is deepest in Life, is a kind of "listening together" with Life Itself. It's intriguing to note that the shape of our inner ear is the same whorling spiral as galaxies. Could it be that our ears are designed for us to listen to and with the cosmos?

One of the most valuable fruits of regular prayer and contemplative practice—both alone and in community—is the inner sanctuary we establish. With this, regardless of what is going on in our lives or in the world, there is a still-point within where we can be nourished and renewed for whatever we are facing, a place we can receive guidance. As we saw in the chapter on Soul Care, this is essential for our activism. It's like the taproot of a tree that allows it to stay anchored even in the fiercest storm, and from which its tendrils reach to entwine with other roots and the mycelial web that undergirds the forest. Really, it is a model for our movements: to root ourselves in the nurturing foundation of Source, and from that place, weave the mycelial networks of our interbeing.

In the unfolding chaos of these times, it is essential to know we are not alone—yet so often we may feel as though we are. It's another both-and: alone and all-one. The intellectual belief in oneness can be helpful to a point, but the real medicine is in feeling our belonging to Life and to one another. A belonging beyond personality or proximity. This also means we will feel the pain around us more acutely—the pain of other people, other life forms, of the planet. And this is where so many of us reflexively disconnect or distract ourselves. But try to stay with it for a bit. Breathe into the collective pain and let it and yourself be held by the larger Breath that breathes you, the Life within and beyond all life. This is the source of our authentic oneness, and of our power to transform the conditions of suffering and injustice. This is the indelible community of our human and more-than-human kin. It extends across time, beyond form and species. Root yourself in this as a lifeline. Listen for it in your bones. It is a daily, moment by moment practice of remembrance and embodiment. It will change you. And you will forget ... and then remember again. That is the journey, and we are on it together.

◎

REFLECTION PRACTICE

One of the listening practices shared in this chapter is consulting the natural world for guidance regarding a particular question or concern. (This practice fits equally well for consulting with the ancestral, elemental, and other relatives discussed in the previous chapter, or with the Divine, however you understand it.) As I suggested above, ideally this can be done outdoors, but if that's not possible you can connect with Nature through your imagination.

- *Begin by writing your question at the top of a clean sheet of paper or in your journal. (Re-read the paragraph above about formulating a generative question.) Your question can be as simple as: What do I need to know right now?*
- *Center yourself in meditation, welcoming only that which is of the highest integrity. Offer a prayer asking to be guided to whoever in the natural world has a message for you in response to your question. As I said, it may be a tree, an insect, an animal, a stone, the wind, or the sun. Something large or small. Everything in Nature is alive and has intelligence. Don't use your mind to figure it out, just be open to where your consecrated attention is called. Then, with humility, ask that entity to share its message.*
- *Next listen. Not just listening with your ears, but with your whole being—attuned to intuitive understandings, images, or other forms of communication. I find it helpful to simply write what I receive, as the scribe, allowing the messenger to write through my pen and onto the page. You can also record the message as a voice memo on your phone, or whatever works best for you. After receiving the*

initial message, you may ask any clarifying questions you have or engage your guide in dialogue.

- *When your session feels complete, thank the messenger and offer a prayer of blessing. Honor the message received—whether it makes sense to you in the moment or not—and trust that deeper dimensions of its meaning will be revealed in time.*

We live in capitalism, its power seems inescapable—but then, so did the divine right of kings. Any human power can be resisted and changed by human beings. Resistance and change often begin in art. Very often in our art, the art of words.

—Ursula K. LeGuin

The world changes according to the way people see it, and if you alter, even but a millimeter the way people look at reality, then you can change it.

—James Baldwin

We have to imagine the kind of society we want to inhabit. We can't simply assume that somehow, magically, we're going to create a new society in which there will be new human beings. No, we have to begin that process of creating the society we want to inhabit right now.

—Angela Davis

12
Dream & Imagine

WHAT IS IT THAT ALLOWS US TO GO A NEW WAY—whether in our personal lives or in the collective life of a city, a nation, or the world? There is an apt metaphor for this transformative process in the lifecycle of the caterpillar and its metamorphosis into a butterfly.

In the mid-1990s I visited a special outdoor exhibit on butterflies at my local Life and Science Museum. The designated area had been turned into a natural habitat incubator with literally hundreds of chrysalises of varied sizes, shapes, and colors hanging like ornaments from the tree branches. They were so plentiful that if you stood in any one place for just a short while, you were certain to witness the process of emergence.

Again and again the arduous birthing was repeated, with these shriveled wet creatures fighting their way free of a self-woven womb that had become their imprisonment. It was like the Nature Channel live, up-close-and-personal. The newly developed beings bore little resemblance to butterflies—they had bloated wet bodies and little stubby wings. But as they pumped the fluid from their swollen bodies into their extending wings, a second metamorphosis took place: one in which they *claimed* their new form in all its power and beauty. And then they flew. The whole process was some serious hard work. Yet without that struggle, their wings would never gain the size and strength necessary to support their new existence.

Caterpillars are eating machines. (If you're a gardener, you probably know this!) They can consume hundreds of times their own weight in a single day, defoliating many plants in the process, before eventually entering into chrysalis. Inside the chrysalis, the caterpillar body breaks down. The same enzymes that enabled their destructive consumption now digest them from within, forming a kind of protoplasmic stew. In that stew are what biologists have poetically named "imaginal cells."[1] It's these cells that carry the pattern for *butterfly*. At first they are destroyed by the immune system as "other" to the self-ness of caterpillar. But as more of them emerge, and especially as they begin to link together, the "self" is redefined—transmuted completely. Imaginal cells are present in the skin of the caterpillar its entire life, but remain dormant until the crisis of breakdown allows them to develop, gradually replacing the caterpillar pattern with the one for butterfly.

What if our destructive over-consuming society is poised for a collective metamorphosis, and each of us is an imaginal cell, holding the blueprint for a new way of being? Perhaps as we come together in the vision of possibility, a momentum is generated, evoking the imaginal as we redefine ourselves and our world. What looks (and no doubt feels) like the worst conceivable outcome for the caterpillar is actually the threshold for an expanded realm of existence: the birth of liberation and flight.

As we experience the massive social and ecological violence unleashed in today's world, I take courage from the parable of the caterpillar, and how its own excesses of consumption ultimately lead to its dissolution and transformation.

There's a parallel here to the archetype of apocalypse: collapse leading to renewal and rebirth. It's *because* of the breakdown (in the caterpillar and in the world) that imaginal cells are activated and catalyze metamorphosis. We can't just build a new world on the infrastructure of the old one. In metamorphosis the caterpillar doesn't simply sprout wings and become a flying caterpillar—it dissolves into formless goo, and from that goo, something entirely new emerges, no longer recognizable as what it was before. The alchemy happens in the liminal space of the in-between.

As the destruction and chaos of apocalyptic times force the collapse of our outworn social structures, we have the opportunity for collective metamorphosis. Some are still trying desperately to resurrect the caterpillar, or pin wings on it, but we can't tinker our way out of a system that was conceived in domination and has genocide at its root. A total dissolution and transmutation is required.

Dreaming Worlds

The great warrior-poet Audre Lorde cautioned that "the master's tools will never dismantle the master's house. They may allow us temporarily to beat him at his own game, but they will never enable us to bring about genuine change." She said, "In a world of possibility for us all, our personal visions help lay the groundwork for political action."[2] Dominant forces stay in power not by convincing people their way is the best way, but by convincing us it's the *only* way. Artists and visionaries are dangerous to the system because they conjure fresh possibilities and offer them as a sacred and subversive medicine, calling us beyond the status quo. Art, music, and writing have the power to transform consciousness, and *that* can transform the world.

Oakland, CA, where I live, is full of dynamic "artivists" whose work combines the arts and activism. Among them is Calvin Williams, a cultural creative, strategist, and young father. He is co-founder of Wakanda Dream Lab, producing immersive world-building and storytelling campaigns for social impact. World-building is a literary technique used in science fiction, speculative fiction, and fantasy to vividly construct the time and place in which a narrative unfolds. We actually engage in world-building all the time, but usually we are re-creating the same dysfunctional world over and over. However, Calvin and his partners use this practice to imagine a whole and thriving world. Their anthology on gender liberation invited "fiction, art, and poetry that was vision-led, future-facing, revolutionary, and social justice oriented" from people across the gender spectrum. Another anthology expanded the possibilities for immigration justice by imagining "love-centered migration and belonging" as the foundation for "new strategies, tactics, and hope for transforming immigration."[3]

Calvin explains, "I believe that visionary fiction offers a framework for narratives that intentionally imagine new possibilities for more just, joyful futures, while also inviting the reader to explore the organizing power to make that possibility into an irresistible material reality."[4] Visionary and speculative fiction invite us into a generative practice. Not necessarily imagining forward to what could be, but writing *from the position of that future*, describing what it's like and how we got there. Such creatives form a visionary vanguard, dreaming new worlds into being and disrupting the dominant narrative.

The United States, and much of the western world, is shaped by a patriarchal white supremacist colonial capitalist imagination. Since the arrival of the first European settlers— and before that on the European continent—governing bodies, the economy, and social infrastructure have been defined by owning class white men. This is the dominant voice on the world stage today, but it doesn't have to be. (And, indeed, it has not always been!) We can activate our own imaginations. Not seeing the world we want to live in, and the self we want to be, as a far-off future destination, but embodying them as a present and ongoing practice.

What would you do differently in the world you are longing for that you might start doing now? What would you *think* differently? One of the ways empire maintains itself is by stifling our ability to dream outside the margins of its prescription, yet it's precisely this capacity that ignites change. A world without fossil fuels. A world without corporations. A world without prisons or police. A world without borders. A world without money. A world without enemies, weapons, or domination. Each of these is possible. When the extent of our innovation is how to modify inherently evil and abusive systems, something has been taken from us—by intention. But we can get it back. By upending what have been considered the "givens" of society, an array of alternatives becomes available.

What is the foundation of your activism? What are the assumptions you may not even be aware of making that limit and define your dreaming? Grace Lee Boggs, whose activism spanned most of her 100 years of life, taught that we must reimagine everything—work, education, community, family, governance—even revolution. In a 2012 dialog with Angela Davis at the annual Empowering Womxn of Color Conference at UC Berkeley, Boggs said, "how we change the world and how we think about changing the world has to change."[5] She suggested we see every crisis as not only a danger, but also an opportunity to become more creative, "to become the new kind of people that are needed at such a huge period of transition."[6] This, she said, is visionary organizing.

Boggs is frequently quoted as observing,

> People are aware that they cannot continue in the same old way but are immobilized because they cannot imagine an alternative. We need a vision that recognizes that we are at one of the great turning points in human history when the survival of our planet and the restoration of our humanity require a great sea change in our ecological, economic, political, and spiritual values.[7]

We can get so focused on the immediate crisis that it's hard to look beyond it. This is another way the status quo is maintained: keeping us so busy putting out fires that we don't have time to dream.

A dozen years ago, or more, I was interviewed for a short video by the Heal the Streets program of the Ella Baker Center for Human Rights. One of the prompts given to me was to describe my vision for Oakland. I was surprised to discover that I didn't have an answer. Bits and pieces, maybe. Or something generically idealistic. But a specific and inspiring prospect for our city—I just couldn't see it. I reflected on the time, energy, and resources that so many of us expend simply trying to survive, trying to undo some of the harshest injustices and maintain even a rudimentary safety net for people in need of support. How much more would be possible if all the energy, the investment of time, attention, and resources that goes into dealing with the daily onslaught of assaults was available for visionary pursuits.

Trauma and exhaustion are stifling to the imagination, and to revolution. It's no accident that the dominant social order keeps Black, Indigenous, and other people of color, LGBTQ+ folks, women, poor and working people, immigrants, and activists traumatized and exhausted. It is a strategy for preserving the existing system. If all our energy is focused on fending off the assaults of injustice, we will be too tired to imagine other possibilities, too tired to fight for them. (Another reason soul care is essential.)

The Nap Ministry was founded by Tricia Hersey to address the generational exhaustion and trauma experienced by Black women under centuries of racial capitalism, and in remembrance of enslaved ancestors who, as she puts it, "had their DreamSpace stolen from them."[8] Her mission is about much more than naps. Rooted in a Womanist and Black Liberation Theological framework, Hersey draws on somatics, the science of sleep, Afrofuturism, and reparations theory to curate spaces of collective care, and collective rest and dreaming, especially for Black women. She explains, "Rest became my refuge and a portal for a connection to my Ancestors. It offered me a place to imagine, heal and be."[9] Her work is not simply about personal renewal; it's fiercely political. Hersey affirms, "Rest is a form of resistance because it disrupts and pushes back against capitalism and white supremacy."[10] She writes, "I am so honored to have the opportunity to hold space for daydreaming, rest, and silence. To imagine a New World that centers liberation, we must practice rest as our foundation to invent, restore, imagine, and build."[11]

Our dreaming of liberative possibilities is not idle, it is profoundly practical. It allows us to see ourselves, one another, and the world in a new way, and thus to act in a new way.

Less than a mile from downtown Oakland, Lake Merritt draws people from all parts of the city to walk, play, gather with friends, celebrate, meditate, and protest. During the racial justice uprisings following the police murder of George Floyd, a memorial altar was constructed at the lake's amphitheater in memory of the Black and Brown lives taken by police and vigilante violence. A caption reads in part, "At a time when the contradictions in our society are laid bare for all to see, we would like to mark this as the beginning of a new era, where the struggle for freedom made a turning point." The text on one side describes the systemic injustice of "The World We Live in Today." Inscribed on the other side is "The World We Wish to See." It reads,

> We wish to live in a world where no one fears that their life may be suddenly taken by another, and people can have faith in strangers. Where every being has access to everything they need to live a fulfilling life without exploiting others. We dream of a world where there is clean air, water, food, and secure and comfortable shelter for everyone. Where all beings are treated with dignity and care, and there is no social hierarchy based on the body they were born into. A world without borders and nations. A world where rest, play, and empathy are deeply valued. A world where people have the autonomy to make decisions for themselves. Now, close your eyes, take a deep breath, and imagine the world you wish to see. What does it look like? What does it feel like? Imagination is the first step to liberation.[12]

I love that it concludes with an invitation to breathe and imagine. It doesn't simply present a vision for others to adopt, but asks "What is the world that *you* would like to inhabit?"— to see it, feel it, breathe into it.

I have always enjoyed word study. There's so much wisdom tucked into the origin and structure of words. The Latin root *spirare* means "to breathe." (This is also related to the word "spiritual.") So to *inspire* is to breathe into or breathe life into, the way the Divine breathes into creation to give it vitality. To *aspire* is to direct one's hopes and dreams toward something. It literally means to breathe upon, the way blowing on embers causes them to burst into flame. To *conspire* is to breathe with or breathe together; to act in harmony toward a shared purpose. There's power and synergy in our breathing together, in our dreaming together, in breathing life into our collective dreams for a more just and harmonious world. A world where our best creative possibilities can flourish.

Models of Transformative Social Change

There are many approaches to social transformation and justice-making: different roles necessary for a comprehensive movement. Exploring some of these models helps to stretch our thinking beyond the common view of activism as only taking place in the streets, the courts, or the halls of government.

Activism can include anything that seeks to change the status quo and shape the foundations of a reimagined world. Of course, this can take place from any position on the political spectrum. Those who overturned voting rights and reproductive justice are activists; however I am concerned here with progressive activism that fosters collective wholeness, and the dignity and well-being of all. At its best activism catalyzes the personal transformation of hearts–minds–souls, and the collective transformation of social structures and institutions. Seen in this way, it can include not only participation in demonstrations and civic actions, but writing, art, music, teaching, healing, praying, farming, parenting, mentoring, creating new systems and ways of being in relationship with one another in the community of Earth.

I've seen several organizations that have each adopted a similar framing, summed up in the alliterative mnemonic Resist, Reform, Reimagine, Recreate. North Carolina-based, Spirit in Action describes these "Four Rs" as the interdependent components of their Theory of Transformation.[13] An illustration on their website places each element within a quadrant of a single circle or wheel. A spiral at the center winds outward and expands through the quadrants, linking them all together and suggesting that they are not so much sequential as simultaneous, synergistic, and evolving. I also see that spiral as symbolizing the spiritual energy that gives life to each approach.

Individuals might feel drawn to different pathways, but each of them has an important function. *Resisters* commit themselves to stopping harm, often by putting their bodies in the way of it. The water and land protectors seeking to stop oil pipelines, tree-sitters acting to halt the clear-cutting of forests, or people chaining themselves as a human barricade to the doors of a financial institution in order to interrupt business as usual are all examples of this. *Reformers* may work within existing institutions to change unjust policies and systems, making them more equitable. *Recreators* generate alternative systems and institutions outside of the dominant structure. And *Reimaginers* envision possibilities for a wholly transfigured world.

We may feel called to work in different areas and with different methods; however all of us are needed and all of our efforts can be part of a single project of wholistic evolution. Particular pathways may resonate with us at different times in our lives, as well. For many years I was involved in street protests and influencing policy before moving into my work as healer, counselor, and retreat leader for front line change-makers— though I still occasionally get out in the streets! Alternately, we might pursue more than one strategy simultaneously to create balance within ourselves. For example, drawing the strength for Resisting through the contemplative inspiration of Reimagining. Whatever the area of our commitment, we can intentionally infuse it (and ourselves) with the vitality and wisdom of the Spirit.

Buddhist scholar, activist, and deep ecologist, Joanna Macy offers another resonant iteration through what she, David Korten, and others have called the Great Turning—the transition from a profit-driven industrial growth-based society toward an Earth-honoring life-sustaining one. If we fail to make the pivot, the Great Turning will become the Great Unraveling, as consumption and extraction exceed capacity, and lead to the end of our human existence on a habitable Earth. There is a clear parallel between Macy's Great Unraveling and Great Turning, and the archetype of apocalypse and apocatastasis we discussed in the first chapter of this book.

At one of her workshops I attended over a decade ago, Macy described the three dimensions necessary to make a shift from the Unraveling toward the Great Turning. While presented as a sequence, they are also simultaneous and mutually reinforcing. As with the Four R's, different people will be working in different arenas toward collective transformation. First *holding* actions to slow the harm to Earth, humans, and all beings. This may save some lives or some ecosystems, Macy said, but of itself is not sufficient. Second is the *creation* of new forms and structures (or the reclamation of ancient ones) that support a life-sustaining society. Permaculture and local currencies are examples of this. These new forms cannot endure, however, without the third component—a shift in collective values and *consciousness* toward a sense of reverence for our mutual belonging to the sacred wholeness of Life.

These models, and others like them, expand the ways we think about social transformation work beyond dualistic confrontational methods, and can transcend the internal movement factions that pit one approach against another. Seeing the important contributions of each strategy means we can value the work of others who may be taking a different approach than our own. Social transformation is an ecosystem within which each element impacts everything in the wider field. I'm using the word "transformation" with intention, rather than simply *change* or *reform,* since change can be changed back. We witness this in the US when a new political party comes into power and un-does the policies of the previous administration, whether through executive order or a stacked Supreme Court. Transformation is wholistic and irreversible. A butterfly cannot go back to being a caterpillar no matter how hard it may try.

The Emerging Beauty

Nature is a wise teacher about the workings of transformation. On a walk in my neighborhood one winter solstice, I was captivated by what the trees were showing me about the turning of cycles, and how it is precisely the energy of new life emerging that hastens the old to its demise. It's not that the old leaves fall and *then* eventually new ones grow in their place. No! It's the emergence of the new leaves that *pushes* the old ones from their branches. Even in winter, when branches are bare, the buds of the coming season are swelling with life.

In these times of upheaval when the old social structures of oppression and inequity are decaying—but still fighting to hold on—it's the new ways of being that we are birthing together that will force empire's inevitable demise. We must not wait until the old ways are gone to dream and build and inhabit the new ones. We can embody them now, as so many are doing. There's great power in the burgeoning life that is steadily pushing forward. And we must honor, with gratitude and humility, that so many of the "new ways" are a return to the wisdom of the Original Peoples of this planet: how to be in community with one another, with Earth and cosmos, with ancestors and coming generations.

A key principle of transformative social change is to focus on vision, rather than the problem. Our work is not just a struggle *against* something, but an ushering in of expansive possibilities for collective flourishing. This is explained beautifully by Akaya Windwood, the former president of Rockwood Leadership Institute, and more recently co-founder of Third Act—a national organization fostering progressive activism among people over sixty. In July 2017, she shared the following social media post:

> Lately I've been experimenting with centering my time and attention on the world so many of us are working hard to create. I imagine it tirelessly—it has become almost a prayer. That world right around the corner whose breath Arundhati Roy hears.[14] Lately I seem to have lost my passion for or even interest in social change—why spend any time changing a dead set of systems that were never meant for most of us? I'd much rather spend my precious time and vital force working toward something I cannot see, can only imagine, but emerges from wholeness and our deepest heart's desire.
>
> These days I'm listening for transformation, where we move not from vanilla to chocolate, but from vanilla to music! I'm willing to take great leaps of faith—to be foolish, wasteful and extravagant in my imagining. It's the only way I can see that will get us through and beyond our current moral and political morass.... Imagining is not mere whistling in the dark—it is a potent act of transformation and world building. It is the process by which we locate our north stars and find our way to liberation.[15]

Sherri Mitchell (Weh'na Ha'mu Kwasset), a spiritual teacher and activist from the Penobscot Nation, points out how much of our focus as activists has historically gone toward creating more inclusion within oppressive systems for people who have been left out, rather than dismantling those systems and actually creating the world we want to inhabit. She has adopted what she calls the 80–10–10 rule. In this, 80% of our energy is devoted to seeding the future we want to live in, with 10% of our time spent paying attention to what is going on in the world, and the remaining 10% invested in stopping harm.[16]

Already people everywhere are reimagining and creating systems for community care and safety, for growing food, generating energy, educating children, exchanging goods and services, settling disputes, and so much more. Guided by Indigenous and ancestral wisdom, these systems are rooted in relationships of mutual collective thriving, not domination and extraction. Another world *is* possible, but she will not arrive on her own. While the implosion of empire may be inevitable, what follows next is not.

Nelson Mandela spoke from experience when he affirmed, "It always seems impossible until it's done." Certainly, the end of the apartheid regime seemed impossible; and his release from prison after 27 years of a life sentence to become president of a multiracial South Africa was nowhere in the realm of prediction. Mandela reminds us not to be limited by what our logic-minds can strategize, not to be bound by the constraints of history or convention, but to dream into the creative expanses that shatter limitations and inspire revolutionary transformation. Yet so many of us have forgotten how to dream boldly, have been trained to dream only within the narrow confines of an immature and individualistic culture.

It can be hard to imagine a different world, especially when we are daily bombarded by the brutal impacts of the dominant paradigm. But dreaming can be courted and cultivated. Look for the evidence. Pay attention to beauty, kindness, and innovation for the collective good. Challenge yourself to stretch your vision beyond harm reduction. (Harm reduction is important, absolutely, but it's not the end point.) What is the world you would truly *love* to inhabit?

The practices throughout this book that invite you into deep listening, into expansive and awe-filled relationships with a larger Life that breathes through the cosmos, will help enlarge your vision and awaken your soul. As Audre Lorde said, "the master's tools will never dismantle the master's house," and neither will the master narrative subvert the dominant paradigm. Through imagination—reaching to the wisdom of ancestors and the dreams of coming generations—we can weave a new narrative upending the worldview of dualistic domination and birthing a world rooted in reverence for the sacred Oneness expressing as all of Life.

REFLECTION PRACTICE

Imagine the beautiful world you haven't yet dared to dream, the world you would truly love to inhabit. Don't worry about it making sense to your logic-mind, or how we might get from here to there. Just be in the future of your sweetest dreaming.

- *What do you see? What is the quality of the light? The colors? The landscape?*
- *What do you hear? Music? Voices? Laughter? The sounds of Nature?*
- *What do you smell? What fragrances are carried on the wind?*

- *What is the taste of the water? Of the air? Of the foods grown from the Earth?*
- *What are the textures and sensations you experience?*
- *How does it make you feel in your emotions? In your soul?*

Allow yourself to tarry in this imagined future, to savor it for as long as you'd like. Return to it regularly, and continue to anchor the feeling of it through your senses into the atoms of your being. Breathe into it. . . . Expand the horizons of possibility.

We know there's no going back to "normal." The path forward demands that we take our rightful places as the younger siblings in creation, deferring to the oceans, forests, and mountains as our teachers.

—Leah Penniman

Since I was very small I have felt that everything, in the natural world, is made of love. As I grew, I realized Love is covered over with hostilities of all kinds. That there is anger, fear, distrust, incessant and unshakeable memory of harm done to us. There is fighting. There is war. However, somewhere, always, there are humans who connect with the intuition I held as a child: that it is all, everything in nature that we see and feel around us, is made of Love.

—Alice Walker

The future is an infinite succession of presents, and to live now as we think human beings should live, in defiance of all that is bad around us, is itself a marvelous victory.

—Howard Zinn

13

Healing the Soul of the World

WHEN I WAS A YOUNG CHILD, I played elaborate games of make-believe with apocalyptic scenarios. The furniture in my bedroom became the rock cliffs I climbed above epic scenes of mass destruction and carnage. My job was to pull survivors from the smoldering wreckage and carry them to safety. To minister to those in pain. Somehow, I didn't feel overwhelmed or inadequate to the task. I knew it was mine to do, and I did it—like any good storybook heroine. There was a sense of exhilaration and purpose in it. Not once did I fear.

Strange, isn't it, that a child of six or seven would play such a game? Where would that come from if not an archetypal awareness; if not the memory-echo of purpose, and the prophetic ancestral whispering of bones? I try to tune into that girl-child, to discover what she understood, and lean into her fearlessness. She was completely invested in acting out the story, but she also knew that just beyond the scenes of chaos, suffering, and destruction was the kitchen, and her mother, and the cat sleeping in a patch of sun.

As seriously as she took the story and her role in it, she knew there was more—another world large and safe enough to hold the drama without being threatened by it. She could give herself to the scene precisely because of the stable world beyond it. The child-me could commit her whole self to the task and not be consumed by it, nor afraid or in despair, because she knew there was something larger that held it. What if we had that same knowledge about our world now? Not diminishing or dismissing the devastation, not distancing from it, but daring to *engage it fully* because we know there is *more*.

Can we give ourselves to the experience of this season on planet Earth? Not using the awareness of something greater as an excuse for spiritual bypass—to avoid facing painful and complex issues—but as the context that allows us to step up and risk everything. What would we do? How would we live? In the swirling current of these cycling times, the simultaneous dying and birthing of worlds, we must feel it and pour out all that is ours to offer, while remembering we are held by something beyond the chaos. A wholeness that is ancient, infinite, and eternal.

We teeter at the threshold of possibility. Collapse of the brutal and bloated system we now inhabit could lead to the birth of beautiful ways of being with one another and Earth.

Or it could lead to unfathomable destruction. Or both. The archetype of apocalypse itself provides a blueprint: collapse and renewal, destruction and creation, death and rebirth. The ending and the beginning spiral into one another.

The beginning *requires* the ending that precedes it. We must die to the illusion of separation and the world it has made. Let. It. Go. Only then can the seeds of the new world solidly take root. This is the initiation we now face, both individually and collectively. There is no way to survive it as who we have been.

Restoring Right Relationships

I once saw a program on the History channel or the Discovery channel, or one of those, about Life After People. It explored the trajectory of Earth if all the people suddenly were gone. They interviewed engineers, scientists, and others who described the rates of decay of man-made structures, the process by which Nature would reclaim cities and towns. It was probably intended to be a cautionary tale, but I found it very reassuring. The animations of crumbling buildings and bridges, of quick growing grasses and trees re-greening the landscape gave me hope! To see that Earth could and would recover in our absence was a gift. The program did not include the variable of nuclear winter, however. It did not conjecture the means by which people disappeared: no tales of pandemics, global warming, nuclear accident, or weapons of mass destruction. Just gone. Earth looked happy as she rapidly recovered and erased most of our "great achievements" with barely a trace remaining. Life surged into fullness and lush adaptive beauty.

We got a small taste of this early in the coronavirus pandemic. When much of the world's human population was sheltering in place—few vehicles on the roads, few ships on the ocean, few planes in the air—Nature quickly responded with dramatically cleaner air and water, and wildlife ventured more freely into urban areas. Residents of Nepal's capital city Kathmandu were able to see Mount Everest, and the Himalayas were visible in parts of India 200 km away for the first time in decades.[1] Dolphins returned to the Bosphorus strait waterway in Istanbul, Turkey, and luxuriant green grass sprouted in urban Italian courtyards usually filled with foot traffic. Skies in Los Angeles were smog-free; many ocean beaches, pristine.[2]

Nature knows how to heal. The same intelligence that reestablishes health in our bodies after illness and mends our broken bones, is always at work in the body of the planet. Ceasing harm and aligning with that intelligence is our most important contribution, so that Nature can do what it *does*. How patient Life is . . . how patient Earth.

Our task is not to "save the planet" (how pompous!) but to restore our right relationship with Earth and all her children, including our human and more-than-human kin. Our task is to put down any notions of superiority, and come in reverent humility to sit at the feet of a Lifeforce that is older and vaster than anything we can imagine.

Perhaps the purpose of coronavirus and climate disasters is about Earth's compassion in trying to awaken us. Again. Still. Louder. To break through our denial of oneness and remind us that we *are* Nature. To get us to realize that unless and until we care for everybody's well-being, "ours" is not secured. As long as we exploit any aspect of Nature, we are assuring our own demise—or that of our children. It's not distant and hypothetical anymore. It is tangible, visceral, now. And still the virus of greed and fear rages in so many, and especially in my white-bodied siblings.

During the early months of covid, mutual aid groups sprang up in communities all over the world. People found purpose and connection through pooling what we had—food, resources, money, skills, information, kindness—and organizing to share it with whoever was in need. We came together to support each other collectively, understanding that our survival depended on one another's, and we found joy in the midst of danger and uncertainty through weaving webs of care. Can you imagine a world where the many trillions of dollars and the considerable amount of human capacity poured into the military, and poured into shoring up an exploitative capitalist market, was invested instead into global mutual aid?

What if we stopped doing what we have proven for centuries now—at horrendous cost—does not work. Redirected this massive focus of time, talent, and treasure into the well-being of people and planet. Everywhere. Without respect to borders or deal-brokering, paternalism, protectionism, extraction, or domination. Just extending genuine care, and whatever resources and support were needed. This would create greater national and international "security" than infinite trillions of dollars toward weapons and walls. (Walls of *all* kinds, literal and metaphorical.) True security, true safety, comes from kinship and belonging.

There is no shortage of resources. There is no shortage of funds. There is no shortage of creativity, capacity, or innovation. It's simply a matter of where it is all being directed. And that is a matter of consciousness. Out of a consciousness of separation, the dominant culture has created a self-amplifying cycle of destruction and consumption that sweeps more and more of everything into its insatiable maw. We are conditioned to believe that this is the inevitable cost of "progress." However, it is neither inevitable, nor progress.

A Transgenerational Project

In times of peril Life calls us into capacities we didn't even know we had. So often we have no idea about the full measure of what we are being called to ... or its consequences. I think that's how Spirit works with us—pretty sneaky, really. "Build an ark,"

Spirit said to Noah—no mention at first of animals gathered, and months at sea with nothing but a thin hope of ever finding land. Just, "Build an ark." "Be the spokesperson for the bus boycott," Spirit told Dr. King when he was a 26-year-old pastor newly arrived in Montgomery, Alabama. "Black lives matter," Spirit said to and through Alicia Garza. "Water is Life," Spirit said to the Lakota and Dakota young people who sparked the peaceful resistance at Standing Rock. "Me too," Spirit told Tarana Burke. "Take a knee," Spirit directed Colin Kaepernick. "Climb a tree," Spirit told Julia Butterfly Hill.

We never really know. I think it's by design, because maybe if we did know what-all we were really agreeing to we would never say yes in the first place. But Spirit and the ancestors lead us in little by little. By the time we realize the magnitude of it we are already committed. It can be costly, but how much more costly if we don't. How tragic to play it safe, to never live into the fullness of our calling.

Healing and liberation are a collective project not an individual one. To meet the challenge will require all of us, and all of our gifts over time. Like the pyramids, the great cathedrals, or the living root bridges of Meghalaya India, this is the work of generations and the work of faith. It was begun by those who came long before us. Each of us is called in turn to lay our stones, to weave our roots, to give our lives toward a purpose larger than we can imagine and whose fruition we may never see. There is no map for these times, and only the compass of our hearts to guide us. Yet there is wisdom in the ancestors' whispering; there is vision in the dreaming of the coming generations. We stand at the nexus between past and future, praying to be faithful to both in the crucial role entrusted to us. And they are with us, urging us on.

There are some dear ones now inhabiting the ancestor realm whose counsel I particularly long for as we face these times. Vincent Harding, who I introduced in the chapter on Soul Care, is at the top of that list. Always a disciple of hope in the midst of tribulation, he saw one of his primary roles as an "encourager." He reminds us,

> We are not alone in this struggle for the re-creation of our own lives and the life of our community. [We] are part of an ageless, pulsating membrane of light that is filled with the lives, hopes, and beatific visions of all who have fought on, held on, loved well, and gone on before us. For this task is too magnificent to be carried by us alone, in our house, in our meeting, in our organization, in our generation, in our lifetime.... We are all a part of one another, and we are all part of the intention of the great Creator Spirit [...] exposing us always to the harsh and the tender, to the dreadful and the compassionate, prying our lives open to the evidence of things unseen.[3]

We need the loving encouragement of elders and ancestors. And we need the beckoning call of coming generations to spur us forward.

In meditation one day I was given a glimpse of the possible world of the yet-to-be-born. It was inspiring, although clearly not guaranteed. Wondering what must happen to reach that future, I was shown that my generational role is more as a death doula to the old world than a midwife to the new, but that I could perhaps offer pre-natal care for the new world as it exists now in its seedling stages. I continue to be very moved by that metaphor. Seedlings are delicate and vulnerable, yet they are tenacious enough to push their way through concrete when they have to.

Curious how this was possible, I did some research. It turns out seedlings don't actually *break* the concrete, *it crumbles around them* as they seek out the moisture in microscopic cracks and extend themselves into those fractures molecule by molecule. This is such a powerful teaching. It's not that we must somehow overpower or "break" empire, but as we nurture the seedlings that emerge from oneness, dualism will crumble. We see it happening already. As empire surges against its inevitable demise, the seedlings for a new world quietly push their way through fissures and cracks in the structures of domination, extending tenacious beauty in the midst of so much horror.

The Way Forward Is Love

I know several women trained as birth doulas and midwives who also work with the dying. It's like they are called to be keepers of the threshold, supporting souls as they move from one dimension to another in either direction. It is a sacred accompaniment. Reflecting on this makes me wonder what such tender ministry might look like in the collective transition we now face. What constitutes a "good death" for a dying planetary epoch, a dying worldview? If the life that we have known is dying, how can we move through the transition with dignity and compassion?

Death doulas see the conscious dying process as an opportunity to reflect on the life we have lived, to harvest our learnings, and perhaps share our insights. It's a time to seek closure and healing in relationships. A time to make amends where we need to, to ask for and offer forgiveness, to say what needs to be said. Approaching death, we might grow mindful of legacy, and choose to live with greater meaning. We may experience a sense of awe and gratitude, savoring the preciousness of small moments. We might feel sadness or regret, resistance and rage, or perhaps relief, acceptance, and peace. Or all of these. We may sense the presence of dear ones who wait for us in the ancestral realm. As we near death, expressing love often becomes the most important thing.

With so much around us dying now, how can all of this guide our way?

The dominant culture regards healing and death as opposites. Yet death can include healing, and healing can, and often does, include death. Sometimes it even requires it. We see this frequently on the personal level, but it's difficult to hold at the planetary scale we are now experiencing. Grappling with this, I sometimes find it hard not to lose faith and get lost in dualisms of my own. I get tangled up in my ruminations, trying to figure out the way through from the rapidly escalating crises of "here" to the beautiful hoped-for possibilities of "there."

Journaling about this a while back, Spirit interrupted me:

You wrestle with yourself so stubbornly, daughter, thinking you have to struggle with a task in order to be faithful. Thinking it is up to you to "figure it out." Thinking. Thinking. If you did less thinking, less figuring, and more allowing, more listening, more opening ... Get out of your own way. What do you know in your bones, daughter?[4]

What arose in me in response was a surprise. It lifted me out of human time and into the cosmic time of our 14-billion-year-old universe. I wrote,

> My bones are of the Earth.
> The same minerals
> as the body of Nature.
> My bones are like the rocks
> embedded in the Earth.
> Ancient. Rooted. Solid.

They have witnessed millennia.
These bones are the bones of the first ancestor,
made of stardust, recycled
and reborn through generations.
They carry memory
of the collapse
and regeneration of worlds,
of destruction and renewal, calamity and hope.
These bones carry
The pain and the wisdom
of the ages. All of it.
One is not superior or
even preferable.
They are conjoined,
like the in-breath and the out-breath.
Both sacred, both essential,
both inherent to Life. One cannot exist
without the other.
Like the *yin-yang* symbol for opposite
yet interconnected forces in Chinese cosmology:
each contains a bit of the other
in an endless dance
of swirling complementarity.[5]

We see it now in the world around us. The dominant force evident is that of destruction, decay, release. But simultaneously, glimpses of new possibilities (the seedlings!) are arising. This is at the heart Thurman's meditation "The Growing Edge": "All around us worlds are dying and new worlds are being born; all around us life is dying and life is being born." Death and regeneration work together! This growing edge, Life's endless innovative expression is, he says, "the basis for hope in moments of despair . . . the source of confidence when worlds crash and dreams whiten into ash."[6]

What's called for is not going back to what has been, as many people seem to think, but gathering up the wisdom of the past, and walking forward through the Mystery into a new manner of being. Nature's own cycles show us the way: turning that which has died (or needs to) into the compost that nourishes emerging life. There is a transformative power available in the midst of apocalypse. It's right that we are here. It's painful and terrifying and achingly hard. However, in this place is our hope. In it is the pivot point toward greater possibility—if we navigate it wisely.

Being courageous doesn't mean we are not afraid. If we weren't afraid, what would we need courage for? Courage is acknowledging the fear and acting anyway. The key to this is in the word itself. The etymological root of "courage" is the Latin word *cor*, which means "heart." Love is what steadies us in the midst of fear, moves us to act in ways we didn't know we were capable of. Love for the Divine. Love for Earth. Love for all our human and beyond-human kin. Love for Life itself.

This time of collapse begs the simple question: What is the world that Love would create? And what is our part—*what is your part*—in bringing it into manifestation? The answer to apocalypse is not technological fixes, but awakening the heart-soul of humanity. We can call to the beauty that is buried in one another and love it into being.

If there is one thing I hope you will take with you from your reading of this book, it is this: *You belong to Life*. You belong to everything and everyone that ever was or will be. You belong to wholeness. And there is nothing that you could ever do, or fail to do, to change this truth. It is only our forgetting that makes it seem so. The healing is in remembrance. This is the medicine for the soul wound of separation. With this awakening, we are empowered by Life itself as agents of collective metamorphosis. We are not here by accident. We are not helpless.

If you are reading these words, you have gifts and purpose that are part of the healing. It may be something you aren't even aware of, or something you take for granted. Or it may be that thing that you have always shied away from, but somehow known was yours to do. It may be something no one ever sees or finds out about, a prayer you offer in the quiet hours before dawn. It may be the way your eyes meet and hold somebody in pain, or the love you give a child. Perhaps a poem or music, or maybe putting your body in the streets as part of a mass movement. Perhaps you grow food in harmony with the Earth, or aid the return of salmon to a river. It is less about the thing than who you become in the doing. The medicine that is needed in the world lives within each of us. We must go deep enough to find it, and bring it forth as our offering to these times.

Additional Spiritual & Healing Practices

Resources to support your ongoing journey ...

SPIRITUAL & HEALING PRACTICES

Audio recordings of several guided healing meditations
are available at: www.lizarankow.org/practices

◎

BREATH & CENTERING PRACTICES

One of the tools I rely on most is the breath. It is always available. First, just finding your breath and *remembering* to breathe is important. Often when we're stressed, anxious, or triggered, we breathe very shallowly or even unconsciously hold our breath. Sometimes we might notice ourselves breathing rapidly. Just pausing to take a slow full intentional deep breath in through your nose, and long slow audible exhalation out through your mouth is a powerful intervention. Slow deep measured breathing can help center you, release stress, and shift the cycle of anxiety. Following, are a number of practices using the breath.

◎

Box Breath

The "box breath" is one simple breath practice. It can be done with your eyes open or closed, depending on what you need to feel safe and comfortable. Think of each component of your breath as the equal side of a box. For example, breathing in for a slow count of four, hold for four, exhale for four, and hold out for four. Sometimes all of that holding can be a challenge, especially if you are just beginning or if you have a medical condition that effects your breathing. So you may want to start with more of a rectangle. Breathe in for a slow count of four, hold for two, breathe out for four, and hold out for two—keeping your attention on the gentle flow of breath in through the nose, and out through the mouth. You can focus on the sensation of the breath at your nostrils, or feel it as it flows down into your belly. Experiment to find what works best for you. You might try increasing the length of each part of the breath, or making your exhalation longer than your inhalation. Some variations suggest making your exhalation twice as long as your inhalation. Practice the box breath, or a variation of it, for a minute, 5 minutes, even 10 or 20 minutes, so it becomes familiar to your body and thus easily accessible in times of need.

Centering Breath Meditation

There are many different ways to meditate. Some involve quiet stillness, others movement or sound. They may be based in a religious tradition, or secular. Some practices incorporate visualization, others a one-pointed focus on breath or a mantra, or perhaps contemplation of a sacred text. Here is a simple centering practice that offers a good place to begin.

Sit with your spine erect, your body in a balanced and comfortable posture. (It may help to stretch and wiggle a bit as you find your position and settle in.) If you are in a chair, have your legs uncrossed and your feet planted on the ground. If you're sitting on the floor or on the Earth, let your sitz bones be the stable point of contact. You can imagine a thread rising from the crown of your head that lifts you gently from above, and passes down, like a plum line, through your body anchoring you deep within the Earth below.

If you are in a place where you feel safe to do so, you may wish to allow your eyes to close. Alternately, you can relax your gaze with a soft downward glance. Either will help you turn your attention inward. Become aware of your breath. Not trying to change it, just noticing its inward and outward flow . . . As you observe your breath, gently allow it to deepen. Not forcing it, but naturally easing into a slower rhythm . . . When your mind starts to wander, softly bring your attention back to your breath, without judgment or duress. (Notice I said *when* your mind starts to wander, not *if.* This is just what the mind does.)

. . . As you continue to simply breathe and *be,* you might have the sense that *Life is breathing you.* Rest in that awareness. Consciously or unconsciously, Life is breathing you, sustaining you, with every moment. Feel the tenderness of that steady support, allowing every breath to infuse you with a sense of deep well-being and peace . . . Continue this practice as long as it feels good to you. When you are ready to bring your meditation to a close, take in a deep vitalizing breath, and gradually return your awareness to your body and the place where you are seated. Carry the feeling of peace within your heart as you (re)enter your day.

◎

Three Blessing Breaths

This is a practice that came to me spontaneously in a group facilitation. It's a good way to open a circle or gathering to help people settle, feel connected, and arrive fully into the space and time. You can also use it on your own, or extend it as a longer solo or group meditation.

Allow your eyes to close, or your gaze to soften with a downward glance (to release any outward distractions). Begin by just noticing your breath, following its gentle flow in, and out. Allow your breath to deepen and become slower, to bring yourself to center.

Now take in a full deep inhalation, breathing in whatever qualities you need in order to be present and nourished in the moment (or for the gathering, workshop, etc.). It may be Peace, Love, Joy, Vitality, Freedom, Harmony, Healing, or whatever you want to call in. On the exhalation, feel and imagine that you are pouring those qualities into your body-mind-and-being, from the crown of your head, to the soles of your feet, to the tips of your fingers. Filling yourself with those energies.

Next breathe in whatever qualities you want to bless the gathering with. Breathe them in on your inhalation, and on your exhalation pour them out to the group. (Or if you are just doing the practice for yourself, continue to breathe in and pour the spiritual qualities or energies that you need into your body-mind-and-being.)

Finally, breathe in whatever spiritual qualities you want to bless the world with, and on your exhalation pour them out to the world.

◎

Healing Presence Breath

Combining breath with intention is a powerful way to bring healing to your body. You can do this practice seated or lying down. I often use it to bring relaxation and healing energy as I go to sleep at night, or in the morning to bring healing and vitality before I get out of bed. It's best if you can be in a safe and quiet place where you will not be disturbed, and where you can allow your eyes to close as you fully relax.

Begin with the Centering Breath Meditation described above. As you breathe, let your body completely relax, feeling a warm wave of comfort or a pleasant tingling sensation spread from the crown of your head, to the soles of your feet, to the tips of your fingers ... Let every breath support you in releasing any stress or tension from your body . . . feel it simply dissolve or drain away.

Allow your awareness to travel gently through your body—from crown to toes to fingertips—noticing any sensations, any places of depletion, congestion, pain, or dis-ease . . . any places in need of care or tenderness. Bring your loving attention, like a healing balm, to every cell in your body, every organ, every bone and muscle, even to the spaces between your cells . . . Take your time with this, and breathe healing energy into your body wherever it is needed . . . You might visualize this energy as a color or colors, or feel it as a pleasant sensation. There are no rules here; trust your body and your intuition to guide you. Just bringing your full *presence* to the tissues of your body can be healing . . . Send love to your body, and gratitude . . .

Tarry with this process as long as it feels good to you, and know that you can return to it at any time . . . When you feel complete, allow your breath to grow stronger as you breathe in a sense of peaceful vitality . . . You may wish to stretch a bit as you return your awareness to your surroundings, and allow your eyes to open.

◎

Loving-Kindness Meditation

Through the teachings of Venerable Thich Nhat Hanh, Loving-Kindness meditation—based on the Buddhist practice of *Metta Bhavana*—has reached far and wide. It's a beautiful way to cultivate compassion for self and others. You may wish to look online to find the practice as it's taught by Nhat Hanh, and the nine prayer statements of benevolence he uses, but here is my own variation. The structure and intention are the same, amplifying the compassionate energy within our hearts and actively extending it as a practice of care.

Before you begin, let me explain the process. There is a set of blessing statements below that you will repeat multiple times, each time directing loving-kindness toward different entities. In the first round the statements are directed toward yourself, for example, *"May I be well, and safe from harm."* Continue from there with the remaining statements of care for yourself, *"May I be . . ."*

Next, you will offer this same set of statements, extending compassionate care toward others, *"May [their name] be . . .,"* beginning with someone you like, then someone about whom you feel neutral, and finally someone with whom you have difficulty. A full set of statements for each. (You can also send blessing to people who have passed away.) If you'd like, you can repeat the practice with groups or nations—starting with the ones you feel positively toward, then neutral, then the difficult ones: *"May they be . . ."* You can even extend this caring energy to Earth, and the many expressions of Nature.

To conclude your session, repeat the set of statements with, *"May all beings be . . ."*

These are not just words that you recite. As you make each statement, visualize the person, group, or entity you are addressing. Allow the genuine feeling of benevolence and care to be what you project outward from your heart *through the vehicle of the words*. It can take practice to develop this spiritual muscle, especially for the people we have difficulty with. But with time, consistency, and intention it will come.

Now, begin with the Centering Breath practice described above. Once you are resting in your inward center, gently bring your attention to your heart. I find it helpful to imagine I am breathing in and out *through* my heart, and with every breath feeling the loving energy within me grow stronger and more radiant.

Following the progression described in the preceding paragraphs, you can make the statements listed below—starting with loving-kindness toward yourself, and continuing from there. These are the prayer statements that were on my heart today. Again, this is my variation on an ancient practice from the Buddha, offered with respect and humility.

> May I be well, and safe from harm.
> May I be peaceful and free from suffering.
> May I feel seen, loved, and cared for.
> May I experience joy each day.
> May I feel my belonging to the wholeness of Life.
> May I live into the fullness of my deepest purpose.
> May I be a beneficial presence to all I touch.

Repeat these prayerful statements for others, as outlined above: *"May [person you have positive feeling for] be peaceful and free from suffering,"* followed by the remaining statements made for that person. Next, *"May [neutral relationship person] be peaceful and free from suffering,"* etc., and then *"May [person with whom you have difficulty] be peaceful and free from suffering,"* etc., and finally, *"May [Group or Nation] be peaceful and free from suffering,"* etc., slowly blessing each person or group as you name them.

To conclude, repeat each statement with *"May all beings . . ."*

◎

Pendulum Breath (aka Mystic Pendulum)

This practice comes from my teacher Brother Ishmael Tetteh in Ghana. I use it routinely to balance and energize myself at the start of the day. Pendulum Breath can also be helpful any time you are feeling anxious, triggered, or depleted. It's a simple yet effective tool.

204 | Additional Spiritual & Healing Practices

You can do this breath practice anywhere. Eyes open or closed. Seated with your spine erect, or standing. It is always available to you. I find it especially powerful to do standing barefoot on the Earth, directly receiving the ministry of Nature and the Elements.

- As you breathe in deeply, imagine yourself rising up into the center of the Sun ... Locate yourself in the center of the Sun ... Feel yourself at one with the Sun, radiant with the Sun's light and power ...

- As you breathe out, let your breath travel down from the Sun, down through the top of your head and through your body ... out the soles of your feet and all the way down into the center of the Earth ...

- Locate yourself at the center of the Earth ... Feel yourself at one with the Earth, rooted in the quiet strength, the deep nurturing peace of the center of the Earth ...

- Then breathe in again, feeling the breath rise up from the center of the Earth, up through your body, up your spine, out the crown of your head, and back up into the center of the Sun ... Again, feel the Sun's radiant Life energy shining as you ...

- Breathe out, and feel the breath moving down from the Sun, down through your body, and back to the center of the Earth ... locating yourself at the center of the Earth ...

Repeat as many times as feels right to you. To conclude, I like to bring both energies—the Sun and the Earth—into balance in my heart.

◎

THE ELEMENTS AS MEDICINE

The Elements are potent spiritual energies. What we touch is the body of each Element, but there is a powerful ancestral spirit within each one as well. Meet them with respect, humility, and gratitude.

The information below is a first aid kit of sorts, that can be particularly supportive for working with trauma and grief, as an adjunct to other care. It's also a resource for ongoing soul care practices, keeping us connected to the larger Life that nourishes all life. As you cultivate your relationship with the Elements, they will teach you their medicine. This list is only to get you started.

Earth

Put your bare feet on the Earth and breathe down through the soles of your feet into the center of the Earth; breathe Her deep peace and nurturance up into you—body, mind, and being. • Lay on the Earth (on your back or belly) and breathe, feel, cry, release, receive. Ask Her to pull out of you whatever does not serve. Pray for it to be transmuted, composted, or turned into flowers. • Get your hands in the soil. Grow plants—garden if you can, but even houseplants are healing companions. • Fragrant herbs and flowers provide living sources of aromatherapy, and there is research showing the antidepressant effects of microbes in the soil. Thank the Earth.

Water

When possible, visit and be with the waters (ocean, lake, river, creek). • Take a spiritual bath or shower. Even an "ordinary" shower can be taken with prayerful intent as spiritual/emotional cleansing, clearing, renewal. Cry, sing, pray in the shower or tub; imagine the water flowing not only over your physical body, but through your energy-body, mind, and emotions as well, washing away anything that needs to be released. Every time you drink water, too, you can affirm this. • Rinsing your hands, face, wrists, neck with cool water can help clear energy you've taken on from others. Flower-water sprays are good for this as well. Thank the Water.

Air

Start with your breath: slow deep nourishing inhalations, long full exhalations. Let your whole body be caressed by every breath. It might make you cry; that's okay. Release what needs to be released. Add sound to it. Sigh loudly, hum, moan, sing. Be present with yourself and keep breathing. • Go outside and feel the fresh air, let the wind blow you clear—body, thoughts, feelings, energy—releasing what you no longer need to carry. Thank the Air.

Fire

Go outside and feel the sun nourishing, recharging, and purifying. Let it shine away or dissolve whatever needs to be released or transformed. Feel yourself radiant with the sun's light and power. • Write down what you want to release and offer it to the flames in a burning ritual. Write down your prayers and offer them, too, to the fire to flow heavenward (or cosmos-wide) on the smoke. Thank the Fire.

NOTES

Chapter 1

1. adrienne maree brown, "Living Through the Unveiling," blog post at http://adriennemareebrown.net/2017/02/03/living-through-the-unveiling/.
2. Michael Meade, "Revelation Again," Living Myth Podcast, episode 213, Feb. 3, 2021. https://www.mosaicvoices.org/episode-213-revelation-again.
3. AnaLouise Keating, "From Borderlands and New Mestizas to Nepantlas and Nepantleras: Anzaldúan Theories for Social Change," *Human Architecture: Journal of the Sociology of Self-Knowledge*, IV, Special Issue, Summer 2006, 9. Learn more about Gloria Anzaldúa's life and work at: https://gloriaeanzaldua.com/.
4. Valarie Kaur speaking at the National Moral Revival Poor People's Campaign Watch Night Service, December 31, 2016.
5. Sonya Renee Taylor, "Radical Self-Love: What It Means for Personal & Collective Liberation." Kripalu webinar, *Amplify Voices of the Global Majority: How We Heal*, May 8, 2025.
6. Rachel Naomi Remen, rachelremen.com. Website home page as archived on November 16, 2022. https://web.archive.org/web/20221116231858/https://www.rachelremen.com/.
7. I first learned about this phenomenon in Howard Thurman's meditation, "The Seed of the Jack Pine," where he uses it as a metaphor for the fires we face in our individual lives. See *Meditations of the Heart* (Friends United Press, 1976), 82–83.

Chapter 2

1. "The Psychology of Purpose" (research review), John Templeton Foundation, February 2018, https://www.templeton.org/wp-content/uploads/2020/02/Psychology-of-Purpose.pdf.

2. "The Psychology of Purpose" (research review), John Templeton Foundation, February 2018, https://www.templeton.org/wp-content/uploads/2020/02/Psychology-of-Purpose.pdf; Laura Anzaldi, "New Movement in Neuroscience: A Purpose-Driven Life," June 1, 2015, https://web.archive.org/web/20211025002310/https://dana.org/article/new-movement-in-neuroscience-a-purpose-driven-life/; Randy Cohen, Chirag Bavishi, and Alan Rozanski, MD, "Purpose in Life and Its Relationship to All-Cause Mortality and Cardiovascular Events: A Meta-Analysis," Psychosomatic Medicine 78, no. 2 (February–March 2016): 122–33; Eric S. Kim et al., "Purpose in Life and Reduced Incidence of Stroke in Older Adults: The Health and Retirement Study," Journal of Psychosomatic Research 74 (2013): 427–32.; Patricia A. Boyle et al., "Effect of Purpose in Life on the Relation Between Alzheimer Disease Pathologic Changes on Cognitive Function in Advanced Age," Archives of General Psychiatry (2012): 499–506. (Note that "correlation" does not confirm a causative relationship, but that these traits are consistently found together.)

3. See, for example, Grace Lee Boggs, *The Next American Revolution: Sustainable Activism for the Twenty-First Century* (University of California Press, 2011).

4. Personal conversation with Howard Thurman quoted by Gil Bailie in his book *Violence Unveiled: Humanity at the Crossroads* (Crossroad Publishing, 1995), xv.

5. Parts of this discussion on Thurman's questions related to purpose are excerpted and adapted from my essay, "Mysticism & Social Action: The Ethical Demands of Oneness," in *Anchored in the Current: Discovering Howard Thurman as Educator, Activist, Guide, and Prophet*, edited by Gregory C. Ellison II (Westminster John Knox Press, 2020), 117–28.

6. Howard Thurman, *Jesus and the Disinherited* (Beacon Press, 1976 [1949]), 110–12.

7. Liza J. Rankow, Journal entry, 2015, in author's possession.

8. Leslee Goodman, "Between Two Words: Malidoma Somé On Rites of Passage," interview in *Sun Magazine*, July 2010, https://www.thesunmagazine.org/issues/415/between-two-worlds.

9. Clarissa Pinkola Estés, "Letter to A Young Activist During Troubled Times," https://www.mavenproductions.com/letter-to-a-young-activist.

Chapter 3

1. Leslee Goodman, "Between Two Worlds: Malidoma Somé on Rites of Passage," *SUN Magazine* (July 2010).

2. Malidoma Somé, *Of Water and the Spirit: Ritual, Magic, and Initiation in the Life of an African Shaman* (Penguin / Arkana, 1994).

3. For more on this see, Malidoma Somé, *The Healing Wisdom of Africa: Finding Life Purpose Through Nature, Ritual, and Community* (Jeremy Tarcher / Putnam, 1998), 285–86.

4. Kazu Haga, *Fierce Vulnerability: Healing from Trauma, Emerging from Collapse* (Parallax Press, 2025), 1.

5. Science and Non-Duality (SAND) conference and film debut, "The Wisdom of Trauma." Opening interview with Dr. Gabor Maté, 6.8.21. For more, see https://thewisdomoftrauma.com. See also Gabor Maté, *The Myth of Normal: Trauma, Illness & Healing in a Toxic Culture* (Avery, 2022), 16–36.

6. Staci K. Hanes, *The Politics of Trauma: Somatics, Healing, and Social Justice* (North Atlantic Books, 2019), 133–47.

7. Goodman, "Between Two Worlds."

8. In 12-step meetings, each time someone speaks they introduce themselves by saying, "I'm John (for example), and I'm an alcoholic." And everyone in the group responds in unison, "Hi, John. Welcome!"

9. Ritual4Return, https://ritual4return.org

10. The term post-traumatic growth was coined by psychologists Richard Tedeschi, PhD, and Lawrence Calhoun, PhD, in the mid-1990s. Their research documented the process through which people who endure psychological struggle following adversity can often see positive growth afterward.

11. Somé, *The Healing Wisdom of Africa*, 277.

12. Michael Meade, *The Water of Life: Initiation and the Tempering of the Soul* (Greenfire Press, 2006). Preface to 2011 edition. (Kindle edition, unpaginated).

13. Dr. Maria Yellow Horse Brave Heart coined the term "historical trauma" to refer to the collective cumulative psychological wounds of massive, repeated, transgenerational group trauma. See Maria Yellow Horse Brave Heart et al., "*Iwankapiya* American Indian Pilot Clinical Trial: Historical Trauma and Group Interpersonal Psychotherapy," *Psychotherapy (Chic)* 57, no. 2 (June 2020): 184–196, doi:10.1037/pst0000267.

14. Arundhati Roy: "The Pandemic Is a Portal" on *Financial Times* website, posted (April 3, 2020), https://www.ft.com/content/10d8f5e8-74eb-11ea-95fe-fcd274e920ca.

Chapter 4

1. Howard Thurman, *Meditations of the Heart* (Friends United Press, 1976), 65–66. (Originally published by Harper & Row, 1953).

2. Thurman, *Meditations*, 65–66.

3. Howard Thurman, *Disciplines of the Spirit* (Friends United Press, 1973), 84. (Originally published by Harper & Row, 1963).

4. Thurman, *Disciplines*, 76. The relevance of this, and of the following paragraph on "changing poison to medicine," to my previous discussion of post-traumatic growth is evident.

5. Viktor E. Frankl, *The Unconscious God* (Washington Square Press, 1985), 137.

6. *SGI Quarterly* (January 2002), https://web.archive.org/web/20060727132550/www.sgi.org/english/Features/quarterly/0201/buddhism.htm.

7. *SGI Quarterly* (January 2002).

8. After devoting himself to the martial arts, training to be a warrior, Morihei Ueshiba ultimately realized that the true way of the warrior is to manifest divine love. For more, see Morihei Ueshiba, *The Art of Peace*, trans. John Stevens (Shambhala, 1992), 6–7.

9. http://www.aikikai.or.jp/eng/aikido/about.html.

10. He spoke of this in his keynote address at a conference of the Agape International Spiritual Center in Los Angeles in 2004.

11. Rachel Naomi Remen, *Kitchen Table Wisdom: Stories That Heal* (Riverhead Books, 1996), 217. Remen's grandfather was a Hasidic rabbi and mystic.

12. Alice Walker, *The Way Forward Is with a Broken Heart* (Ballantine Books, 2000), 200.

13. Cat Brooks et al., "Oakland Is Reimagining Public Safety," Anti Police-Terror Project, 2021 report, version 2.0, www.antipoliceterrorproject.org/oakland-is-ready-to-reimagine-public-safety.

14. For examples of this organizing, see https://defundpolice.org/ and https://criticalresistance.org/about/history/.

15. Martin Luther King, Jr., "Beyond Vietnam: A Time to Break the Silence," sermon given on April 4, 1967, at Riverside Church in NYC. A year later, to the day, King was assassinated. The sermon was drafted primarily by Dr. Vincent Harding.

16. Interview with James Baldwin, "The Doom and Glory of Knowing Who You Are," *Life Magazine*, May 24, 1963, https://www.brainpickings.org/2017/05/24/james-baldwin-life-magazine-1963/ and https://medium.com/the-1000-day-mfa/unprecedented-in-the-history-of-the-world-49bc965a7305.

17. Barbara A. Holmes, *Crisis Contemplation: Healing the Wounded Village* (Center for Action and Contemplation, 2021), 95.

18. Sobonfu Somé, "Embracing Grief," http://www.sobonfu.com/articles/writings-by-sobonfu-2/embracing-grief/.

19. Angela W. Buchdahl, "Nothing More Whole than a Broken Heart," sermon for Rosh Hashanah 5578 (September 20, 2017), https://www.centralsynagogue.org/worship/sermons/nothing-more-whole-than-a-broken-heart-rosh-hashanah-5778.

Chapter 5

1. Estelle Frankel, *Sacred Therapy: Jewish Spiritual Teachings on Emotional Healing and Inner Wholeness* (Shambhala Publications, 2003), 4. For more on her work, see http://www.estellefrankel.com.

2. Cara Page and Erica Woodland, *Healing Justice Lineages: Dreaming at the Crossroads of Liberation, Collective Care, and Safety* (North Atlantic Books, 2023), 4.

3. Parts of this paragraph are adapted from my profile of the Hardings on the website for OneLife Institute, https://www.onelifeinstitute.org/shoulders-we-stand-on. For more about their work see: www.vohp.org.

4. Shawn Ginwright, "The Future of Healing: Shifting from Trauma Informed Care to Healing Centered Engagement," posted May 21, 2018, https://ginwright.medium.com/the-future-of-healing-shifting-from-trauma-informed-care-to-healing-centered-engagement-634f557ce69c. He has since published a related book, *The Four Pivots: Reimagining Justice, Reimagining Ourselves* (North Atlantic Books, 2022).

5. This quote was something Kazu posted on social media around 2015 that was turned into a meme and circulated widely on the internet. He subsequently made a similar statement in his book *Healing Resistance: A Radically Different Response to Harm* (Parallax Press, 2020), 32.

6. Parts of this discussion on self-care and soul care are excerpted and adapted from my essay, "Mysticism & Social Action: The Ethical Demands of Oneness," in *Anchored in the Current: Discovering Howard Thurman as Educator, Activist, Guide, and Prophet*, edited by Gregory C. Ellison II (Westminster John Knox Press, 2020), 117–28.

7. Sustaining the Soul of Activism was launched in 2010. For more, visit https://onelifeinstitute.org/sustaining-activism.

8. For more, see https://www.nodaplarchive.com/.

9. Lyla June Johnston's video message is reposted at https://healingheartsatwoundedknee.com/its-time-to-pray-standing-rock/.

10. Mushim Ikeda, "I Vow Not to Burn Out," in *Lion's Roar: Buddhist Wisdom for Our Time*, https://www.lionsroar.com/i-vow-not-to-burn-out/. Additional info, see https://eastbaymeditation.org.

11. Resmaa Menakem, *My Grandmother's Hands* (Central Recovery Press, 2017), 139.

12. Dacher Keltner, *Awe: The New Science of Everyday Wonder and How It Can Transform Your Life* (Penguin Press, 2023), 11.

13. Keltner, *Awe,* 11.

14. Keltner partnered with Mindful.org to create a four-minute video of a guided awe walk in Muir Woods with a 360-degree virtual reality feature that allows you to look up, down, left, or right to change the view of the video (https://youtu.be/TKter wanr1Y?si=1FwJWBj2ooNyt68D). The Greater Good Science Center at the University of California Berkeley offers a number of resources for cultivating awe. Among these is a quiz to measure your own awe quotient (https://greatergood.berkeley.edu/quizzes/take_quiz/awe).

15. https://www.universityofcalifornia.edu/news/awe-walks-boost-emotion.

16. https://www.universityofcalifornia.edu/news/dacher-keltner-awe-inspired-and-you-should-be-too.

Chapter 6

1. Technically speaking emotions and feelings are not the same. There is a whole scientific literature breaking this down, but since, in common parlance, we most often use the terms interchangeably, I will follow that convention here.

2. Mark Nepo, *The Book of Awakening: Having the Life You Want by Being Present to the Life You Have* (Conari Press, 2000), 18.

Chapter 7

1. John Polkinghorn, *Science and Theology: An Introduction* (Fortress Press, 1998), 31.

2. Daniel Matt, "Nonduality," in *The Essential Kabbalah* (HarperSanFrancisco, 1995), 24.

3. Liza J. Rankow, "Mysticism & Social Action: The Ethical Demands of Oneness," in *Anchored in the Current: Discovering*

Howard Thurman as Educator, Activist, Guide, and Prophet, edited by Gregory C. Ellison II (Westminster John Knox Press, 2020), 119.

4. https://www.therightsofnature.org/ecuador-rights/ (italics in the original). Since that time, other countries and municipalities have adopted similar measures. To be clear, it's not that humans *gave* these rights to Nature, but rather recognized the inherent rights of the natural world.

5. The 2010 Supreme Court decision in *Citizens United v. Federal Election Commission* codified this.

6. "The 'Great Replacement' Theory, Explained," https://immigrationforum.org/wp-content/uploads/2021/12/Replacement-Theory-Explainer-1122.pdf; https://www.splcenter.org/hatewatch/2022/05/17/racist-great-replacement-conspiracy-theory-explained; https://www.goodreads.com/en/book/show/15705124-le-grand-remplacement; https://en.wikipedia.org/wiki/Renaud_Camus#The_Great_Replacement

7. In one of the variations of Replacement Theory, Jewish elites are the ones responsible for the plot to replace the culture and political power of white people in the US and Western Europe. "The 'Great Replacement' Theory, Explained," op cit.

8. For more on the brain science, see, for example, https://study.com/academy/lesson/the-amygdala-definition-role-function.html.

9. Howard Thurman, *Jesus and the Disinherited* (Beacon Press, 1976), 44. (Originally published by Abingdon-Cokesbury, 1949.)

10. Commonly attributed to Mahatma Gandhi, but an original source could not be verified.

11. Mumia Abu-Jamal, *Death Blossoms: Reflections from a Prisoner of Conscience* (Plough Publishing House, 1997), 36–37.

12. The term "kin-dom" was introduced by Ada María Isasi-Díaz in *Mujerista Theology* (Orbis Books, 1996), 89.

13. Rankow, "Mysticism & Social Action," 120.

14. Jean Houston, *A Mythic Life: Learning to Live Our Greater Story* (HarperSanFrancisco, 1996), 65.

15. Thomas Merton, in *The Essential Writings of Thomas Merton,* edited by Christine M. Bochen (Orbis Books, 2000), 90, 92.

Chapter 8

1. Kaiser Irani, *Avadhoot of Arbudachal: A Biography of Vimala Thakar.* (Prabhat Printing Works, 2004), 25–26. This and many of her books are available as PDF downloads here: https://vimalathakar.world/books/.

2. Vimala Thakar, *Spirituality and Social Action: A Holistic Approach* (Vimala Programs California, 1984). Excerpted online at https://vimalathakar.com/who-is-vimala-thakar/.

3. Later I discovered the same term used by Alton Pollard in his book *Mysticism and Social Change: The Social Witness of Howard Thurman* (1992), and related concepts in the work of theologians Beverly Lanzetta, Janet Ruffing, and Dorothee Soelle.

4. Howard Thurman, "Mysticism and Social Action," Lawrence Lecture on Religion and Society, First Unitarian Church of Berkeley, Kensington, CA, October 13, 1978.

5. Thurman, "Mysticism and Social Action."

6. Desmond Tutu, "Where Is Now Thy God?" (address), Trinity Institute, NY, January 8, 1989, quoted in Michael Battle, *Reconciliation: The Ubuntu Theology of Desmond Tutu* (The Pilgrim Press, 1997), 47.

7. Desmond Tutu, *God Has a Dream* (Doubleday / Random House, 2004), 49–50.

8. Desmond Tutu, "The New World Order." Paper in absentia, the International Foundation for Socio-Economic and Political Studies, Moscow Conference, July 14–15, 1992, quoted in Battle, *Reconciliation*, 35.

9. Desmond Tutu, "My Credo," in *Living Philosophies: The Reflections of Some Eminent Men and Women of Our Time*, edited by Clifton Fadiman (Doubleday, 1990), 235, quoted in Battle, *Reconciliation*, 48.

10. https://kinginstitute.stanford.edu/encyclopedia/southern-christian-leadership-conference-sclc.

11. Martin Luther King, Jr., *Strength to Love* (Philadelphia: Fortress Press, 1981), 27.

12. https://www.americanrhetoric.com/speeches/mlkatimetobreaksilence.htm.

13. Henri J. M. Nouwen, *The Wounded Healer* (Doubleday, 1972), 19.

14. For more, see https://www.sarvodaya.org/.

15. In his 1978 Lawrence Lecture, "Mysticism and Social Action," Thurman relates the story shared with him by his friend and colleague Reinhold Neibuhr, of a young man attending one of Neibuhr's lectures who approached him afterward to opine, "When this Thurman fellow came up out of Florida and began to talk around, many of us who were much younger were sure that at last someone had come who would be our Moses. And what did he do? He turned mystic on us!"

16. Vincent G. Harding, Liza J. Rankow, Luther E. Smith, and Olive Thurman Wong, eds., *The Living Wisdom of Howard Thurman: A Visionary for Our Time,* audio collection (Sounds True, 2010). The original title of the sermon was "Men Who Walked with God" preached April 12,1953, at Fellowship Church in San Francisco, CA.

17. Thich Nhat Hanh, *Peace Is Every Step* (Bantam Books, 1991), 103.

18. Karin Lofthus Carrington and Susan Griffin, eds., *Transforming Terror: Remembering the Soul of the World*, Shantideva's Prayer (University of California Press, 2011), 100.

19. Vimala Thakar, "Awakening to Total Revolution—Enlightenment and the World Crisis," in *Spirituality and Social Action: A Holistic Approach* (Vimala Programs California, 1984), available at https://www.scribd.com/document/372543555/Vimala-Thakar-Awakening-to-Total-Revolution-Enlightenment-and-the-World-Crisis.

20. Thakar, "Awakening to Total Revolution."

21. Thakar, "Awakening to Total Revolution."

22. Thakar, "Awakening to Total Revolution."

23. bell hooks, "Love as the Practice of Freedom" in *Outlaw Culture* (Routledge, 1994), 250.

24. Gloria E. Anzaldúa, *Light in the Dark / Luz en lo Oscuro: Rewriting Identity, Spirituality, Reality*, edited by AnaLouise Keating (Duke University Press, 2015), 138.

Chapter 9

1. Not all Europeans were accepted into whiteness in the beginning—Irish, Italians, and Jews were among those excluded and each regarded as a separate inferior race. But over time they, too, were brought into the fold as a way to build the numbers and increase the power base of whiteness, and to preempt their making common cause with Black and other people of color in movements for social and economic justice.

2. Resmaa Menakem, "Healing Your Thousand-Year-Old Trauma," posted June 7, 2018, at https://medium.com/@rmenakem/healing-our-thousand-year-old-trauma-d815009ae93.

3. For a helpful exploration of these and related issues, see Jesse A. Myerson, "White Anti-Racism Should Be Based in Solidarity Not Altruism," *The Nation*, February 5, 2018, https://www.thenation.com/article/activism/white-anti-racism-must-be-based-in-solidarity-not-altruism./

4. Fosl, Catherine. "'There Was No Middle Ground': Anne Braden and the Southern Social Justice Movement." *NWSA Journal* 11, no. 3 (1999): 24–48. http://www.jstor.org/stable/4316680.

5. For an excellent summary of the history of whiteness, see the essay "Roots Deeper Than Whiteness" by David Dean on the White Awake archival website https://whiteawakearchive.org/2018/10/27/roots-deeper-than-whiteness/. See also Jacqueline Battalora, *Birth of a White Nation: The Invention of White People and Its Relevance Today* (Strategic Book Publishing and Rights Company, 2013), 36.

6. The legacy of the Doctrine of Discovery continues to impose devastating impacts around the world. Learn more at https://aila.ngo/wp-content/uploads/2022/05/Doctrine-of-Discovery-Booklet-rev3.1.pdf.

7. For more on this, see Lyla June Johnston, "The Story of How Humanity Fell in Love with Itself Once Again," https://whiteawakearchive.org/2018/01/31/the-vast-and-beautiful-world-of-indigenous-europe/; John Philip Newel, *Sacred Earth, Sacred Soul: Celtic Wisdom for Reawakening to What Our Souls Know and Healing the World* (HarperOne/HarperCollins Publishers,

2021); Riane Eisler, *The Chalice and the Blade: Our History, Our Future* (HarperCollins Publishers, 1987). Also of interest, see https://decolonialatlas.wordpress.com/2018/03/17/european-paganism-and-christianization/.

8. Learn more about this work at https://stirfryseminars.com/products/the-color-of-fear-part-one/.

9. If you are unfamiliar with the history, scope, and impact of what were called the Indian Residential Schools, you can begin to learn more at https://www.pbs.org/articles/the-history-and-impact-of-residential-schools.

10. Aurora Levins Morales, *Medicine Stories* (South End Press, 1998), 76–77.

11. Grassroots Reparations website: https://thetruthtellingproject.org/grc/.

12. The term "soul wound" was introduced in the context of intergenerational racial trauma by Indigenous psychologist Dr. Eduardo Duran (Tiospaye Ta Woapiye Wicasa) in his book, *Healing the Soul Wound: Trauma Informed Counseling for Indigenous Communities* (Teacher's College Press, 2019).

13. Kelly Brown Douglas, "A Christian Call for Reparations," *Sojourners*, July 2020, https://sojo.net/magazine/july-2020/christian-call-case-slavery-reparations-kelly-brown-douglas.

14. Nate Lee, "Liberative Kinship: Black Lives, the Asian Diaspora, and an Already Looted World," https://www.inheritancemag.com/stories/liberative-kinship.

Chapter 10

1. Drew Dellinger, "hieroglyphic stairway," in *love letter to the milky way: a book of poems* (White Cloud Press, 2011), 3.

2. Robin Wall Kimmerer, "Building Good Soil," in *What Kind of Ancestor Do You Want to Be?*, edited by John Hausdoerffer et al. (University Chicago Press, 2021), 182.

3. Kimmerer, "Good Soil," 183.

4. Omid Safi, Religion News Service blog, January 27, 2014, https://web.archive.org/web/20150523062503/http://omidsafi.

religionnews.com/2014/01/27/need-die-now-die-die-braveheart-garth-brooks-living-now-according-prophet-muhammad/. Also see https://www.huffpost.com/entry/rumi-the-meaning-of-life-and-death_b_1391215.

5. Graham Robb, *The Discovery of Middle Earth: Mapping the Lost World of the Celts* (W. W. Norton, 2013), 286.

6. Joel Goldsmith made this the title of his 1964 book *A Parenthesis in Eternity*. Deepak Chopra uses the term in his 1994 book *The Seven Spiritual Laws of Success*. But the phrase dates back much farther than either of these. Multiple authors cite the 17th-century use of the phrase by Sir Thomas Browne.

7. Howard Thurman, "A Good Death," in *The Inward Journey* (Friends United Press, 1971), 25. (Italics in the original.)

8. Thurman, "A Good Death."

9. Howard Thurman, "A Tribute to Life," excerpt from sermon "The Quest of the Human Spirit" (1962), in *The Living Wisdom of Howard Thurman*, audio collection. (Sounds True, 2010).

10. Credo Mutwa, "A Message for the World," interview by Global Oneness Project, https://www.youtube.com/watch?v=Vv3R6hddPfI&. Baba Mutwa joined the ancestors in 2020 at the age of 98.

11. Layla F. Saad, blog post January 17, 2021, http://laylafsaad.com/letters-from-layla/is-this-helping-me-become-the-good-ancestor-i-want-to-become.

Chapter 11

1. Even if we stopped all carbon emissions completely *today*, stopped all wars, there is a huge amount of destruction already baked into the system. Species extinct. Languages and the insights they hold, lost. Warm oceans choked with plastic. Stockpiles of nuclear waste and weapons. This is not a reason to give up, however, but an indication of urgency.

2. Dorothee Soelle, *The Silent Cry: Mysticism and Resistance* (Fortress Press, 2001), 74.

3. Mark Nepo, *The Exquisite Risk* (Three Rivers Press, 2005), 3.

4. Ranier Maria Rilke, *Letters to a Young Poet* (W. W. Norton, 1954 [1934]), 35.

5. Glen Clark, *The Man Who Talks with the Flowers: The Life Story of Dr. George Washington* Carver (Macalaster Park Publishing, 1994 [1939]), 22.

6. Parker Palmer, *A Hidden Wholeness: The Journey Toward an Undivided Life* (Jossey-Bass, 2004), 134. A helpful video on "Using Evoking Questions for Deeper Listening" is here: https://youtu.be/P2iv3YHb9sY.

7. Parker Palmer, "The Clearness Committee: A Communal Approach to Discernment," https://couragerenewal.org/wp-content/uploads/2022/06/Parker-Palmer_Clearness-Committee.pdf.

8. "Conversations with Howard Thurman," video interview, part 2, https://youtu.be/NPsZBS-2oeU.

9. As an example, here's a prayer I recorded some years back and shared on YouTube: https://youtu.be/UyrPhwLuPJo?si=vt71tHKQ0OphpPp4.

10. Desmond M. Tutu, *God Has a Dream: A Vision of Hope for Our Time* (Doubleday, 2004), 103.

11. Howard Thurman, "Mysticism and Social Action," Lawrence Lecture on Religion and Society, First Unitarian Church of Berkeley, Kensington, CA, October 13, 1978, 17.

Chapter 12

1. The scientific meaning of the term refers to the "imago," the mature adult insect produced after metamorphosis, but the metaphorical poetics of it are inspiring! I first learned about this process, and the role of imaginal cells, from futurist and evolution biologist Dr. Elisabet Sahtouris, in the early 2000s. She also offers it as a parable for the times we inhabit.

2. Audre Lorde, *Sister Outsider: Essays and Speeches* (Crossing Press, 1984), 110–14.

3. *Black Freedom Beyond Borders: A Wakanda Immigration Anthology*, Wakanda Dream Lab, 2018, https://www.wakandadreamlab.com/wakanda-dream-lab-anthology.

4. "Freedom Dreaming: Calvin Williams Answers Your Questions on Afrofuturism." Institute for the Future, September 29, 2021, https://www.iftf.org/insights/freedom-dreaming-calvin-williams-answers-your-questions-on-afrofuturism/. "Visionary fiction" is a term coined by adrienne maree brown and Walidah Imarisha to describe writing that engages a radical imagination of liberated futures, inviting readers into a world that does not yet exist. (See their anthology *Octavia's Brood*, AK Press, 2015.)

5. A partial transcript of Boggs's remarks was published in *Race, Poverty & the Environment*, 19 no. 2 (2012): 44–45. Video of the full event is at https://www.youtube.com/watch?v=h9IsJwE0B1c.

6. Boggs in *Race, Poverty & the Environment*.

7. "From Banks and Tanks to Cooperation and Caring: A Strategic Framework for a Just Transition," Movement Generation Justice and Ecology Project. November 2016, 4–6, https://movementgeneration.org/justtransition/.

8. Tricia Hersey blog post, "Rest is anything that connects your mind and body," February 2022, https://thenapministry.wordpress.com/2022/02/. For more on Hersey and her work, see https://thenapministry.wordpress.com/about. Since this time, Hersey's bestselling book *Rest Is Resistance: A Manifesto* was published (Hachette, 2022).

9. Hersey blog post, "The Future Is Now: Why Octavia Butler is Our Muse," April 2020, https://thenapministry.wordpress.com/2020/04/.

10. Hersey blog post, "Slowly Emerging After a 3 Week Sabbath," July 2020, https://thenapministry.wordpress.com/2020/07/.

11. Hersey blog post, "Resources from 'A Space to Rest' Virtual Experience," August 2020, https://thenapministry.wordpress.com/2020/08/.

12. Memorial altar installation at Lake Merritt amphitheater, Oakland, CA, Summer 2020.

13. Spirit in Action, https://spiritinaction.net/about-us/our-approach/. The organization NC Climate Justice Collective credits their co-founder Jodi Lasseter as the creator of the framework, https://www.ncclimatejustice.info/our-approach

14. This is a reference to the quote by writer and activist Arundhati Roi, "Another world is not only possible, she is on her way. On a quiet day, I can hear her breathing." Arundhati Roi, *An Ordinary Person's Guide to Empire* (South End Press, 2004), 86.

15. Akaya Windwood, Facebook, July 3, 2017, reprinted with permission. Windwood has since published *Leading with Joy*, coauthored by Rajasvini Bhansali (Berrett-Koehler Publishers, 2022).

16. Sherri Mitchell, *Sacred Instructions: Indigenous Wisdom for Living Spirit-Based Change* (North Atlantic Books, 2018), 139.

Chapter 13

1. https://www.insider.com/photos-videos-earth-planet-thriving-coronavirus-2020-4#in-india-the-himalayas-were-visible-for-the-first-time-in-decades-13.

2. https://www.loveexploring.com/galleries/96018/incredible-images-that-show-how-the-earth-is-healing-during-coronavirus.

3. "We Are Not Alone," quote from Vincent Harding. This is found several places online without indication of the original source, and nobody I reached out to, including Dr. Harding's daughter (herself a noted scholar) had additional information. She thought it sounded like a transcription of oral remarks he made. The website for Radical Discipleship had the most complete version, but they were also unable to provide the source. Https://radicaldiscipleship.net/2015/01/10/1280/. Brackets and ellipses in the online version, except the final [...] which is my edit for clarity and flow.

4. Liza J. Rankow, Journal entry, January 7, 2022, in author's possession.

5. Rankow, Journal entry, January 7, 2022.

6. You can find the full meditation as the epigraph for this book. It is from Howard Thurman, *Meditations of the Heart* (Friends United Press, 1976), 134.

ACKNOWLEDGMENTS

I am often in awe of the amazing people in my life.

I'm a better human because of the generous friendship of Vincent Harding, Alice Walker, Rev. Deborah L. Johnson, Michelle Alexander, and Barbara A. Holmes. Each of them has not only contributed to my thought and writing over many years, but to the richness of my living. Alice and Michelle each read early portions of this work, and both Deborah and Barbara slogged their way through the first full draft. All provided loving encouragement and valuable feedback.

Many spiritual teachers have shaped me over my lifetime; I am indebted to all of them. Two who have been among my deepest anchors are Dr. Howard Thurman and Brother Ishmael Tetteh. Even when they are not named in this text, their imprint is present.

And there are so many cherished souls who have companioned and sustained me along the way—friends, chosen and biological family, community members, colleagues, counseling clients, students, retreat participants, movement activists, writers, musicians, artists, thinkers, elders, children, healers, and all the extraordinary ordinary people who inspire me daily. It's a cliché to say there is no way to name them all, but it's true. A deep bow (and a warm hug) of gratitude.

Endless thanks to the entire team at Orbis Books. To Robert Ellsberg, for his immediate and supportive interest in the project. To Maria Angelini for working magic to keep everything on track. And above all to my editor, Lil Copan. Truly, this is a better book because of her care and skill.

Thank you to Joelle Hanh and Nirmala Nataraj for early editorial guidance that helped me become a more competent writer.

Special appreciation to everyone who provided an endorsement blurb for this book. I honestly don't think any of them had time to do it, yet they did. And I am so honored.

Thank you to Laura Loescher for use of her Earth Altar image, "Collaboration," that graces the cover of this work.

First, last, and always, my whole heart and soul in gratitude to the Infinite Sacred Life that breathes through all that is. To this precious and beautiful Earth. To all who guide us from the Ancestral realm. And to the generations yet to come.

INDEX OF SPIRITUAL & HEALING PRACTICES

Ancestral Altar, 83–84, 90

Ancestral Breath, 148–149

Awe, 73–76

Box Breath,* 197–198

Centering Breath Meditation,*
198–199

Clearness Committee, 159–160

Dreaming the Possible World,
181–182

Elements as Medicine,*
205–206

Emotions Altar, 86, 90

Emotions (Dialogue with),
84–86

Healing Presence Meditation,*
200–201

Inner Child and Inner Elder,
80–82

Inner Listening (Discernment),
154–158

Life Review (Death as Ally),
142–143, 145, 150–151

Life's Working Paper, 19–20

Loving-Kindness Meditation,*
201–203

Medicine in Our Wounds, 54,
58–59

Mystic Activism, 121

Nature as Oracle, 158–159,
165–166

Pendulum Breath,* 203–204

Prayer, 161–163

Purpose (Discerning Soul's
Purpose), 16, 18-21, 26

Soul Care, 66–67, 75–77

Spiritual 911, 69–70, 76–77

Spiritual Jogging Partner,
160–161

Three Blessing Breaths,*
199–200

Wilderness Times, 8–9, 13–14,
42

Described in full in the appendix.